HOW TO
SAVE A LIFE

Lynette Rice

HOW TO SAVE A LIFE

THE INSIDE STORY OF GREY'S ANATOMY

HEADLINE

First published in the UK in 2021
by HEADLINE PUBLISHING GROUP

2

Cataloguing in Publication Data is available from the British Library

Hardback ISBN 978 1 4722 9031 1
Trade paperback ISBN 978 1 4722 9032 8
Ebook ISBN 978 1 4722 9034 2

Offset in 11/18 pt ITC Giovanni Std by Jouve (UK), Milton Keynes

Printed and bound in Great Britain by Clays Ltd, Elcograf S.p.A.

Design by Meryl Sussman Levavi

HEADLINE PUBLISHING GROUP
An Hachette UK Company
Carmelite House
50 Victoria Embankment
London
EC4Y 0DZ

www.headline.co.uk
www.hachette.co.uk

Contents

9

"It's a Beautiful Day to Save Lives,"
Or, The Guest Stars Who Survived and Those Who Didn't

151

10

"Somebody Sedate Me,"
Or, How *Grey's Anatomy* Managed to Gross You Out

165

11

"Not Everyone Has to Be Happy All the Time.
That Isn't Mental Health. That's Crap,"
Or, Eleven of the Most Memorable Episodes of *Grey's Anatomy*

183

12

"Trauma Always Leaves a Scar,"
Or, The Most Heartbreaking Departures and Deaths

209

Interlude
"Keep Breathing" by Ingrid Michaelson

237

13

"We Have to Keep Reinventing Ourselves, Almost Every Minute,
Because the World Can Change in an Instant,"
Or, How Shonda Rhimes and Ellen Pompeo Became
the Highest-Paid Women in Television

243

14

"Everybody Wants Their Place in History,"
Or, Deciding When to Hang Up the Scrubs
271

Author's Note

Summarizing seventeen seasons of *Grey's Anatomy* is almost as difficult as performing a Whipple procedure, so I decided to pay tribute to TV's longest-running medical drama by zeroing in on specific themes, moments, and certain unforgettable stars. To achieve that, I interviewed nearly eighty actors, writers, directors, producers, crew members, and executives over the course of twelve months and one rather nasty pandemic. Not everyone was available due to scheduling and, for a few, because of the extraordinary influence (actual or perceived) of the ever-private Shonda Rhimes. (In fact, here's an actual quote from when I was declined one interview: "No one wants to piss her off.") So, for those who were unavailable, including Shonda, I relied on archival interviews that I and some of my colleagues had conducted over the years for *Entertainment Weekly* magazine. A full list of stories that I drew from is provided at the back of the book.

Cast of Characters

The Actors

ELLEN POMPEO
(Dr. Meredith Grey, 2005–present)

PATRICK DEMPSEY
(Dr. Derek Shepherd, 2005–2015)

SANDRA OH
(Dr. Cristina Yang, 2005–2014)

ISAIAH WASHINGTON
(Dr. Preston Burke, 2005–2007, 2014)

KATHERINE HEIGL
(Dr. Izzie Stevens, 2005–2010)

T. R. KNIGHT
(Dr. George O'Malley, 2005–2009)

JUSTIN CHAMBERS
(Dr. Alex Karev, 2005–2020)

JAMES PICKENS, JR.
(Dr. Richard Webber, 2005–present)

CHANDRA WILSON
(Dr. Miranda Bailey, 2005–present)

KATE WALSH
(Dr. Addison Montgomery, 2005–2012)

SARA RAMIREZ
(Dr. Callie Torres, 2006–2016)

ERIC DANE
(Dr. Mark Sloan, 2006–2012)

BROOKE SMITH
(Dr. Erica Hahn, 2006–2008)

KEVIN McKIDD
(Dr. Owen Hunt, 2008–present)

JESSE WILLIAMS
(Dr. Jackson Avery, 2009–present)

SARAH DREW
(Dr. April Kepner, 2009–2018)

KIM RAVER
(Dr. Teddy Altman, 2009–2012, 2017–present)

JESSICA CAPSHAW
(Dr. Arizona Robbins, 2009–2018)

JASON GEORGE
(Dr. Ben Warren, 2010–present)

CATERINA SCORSONE
(Dr. Amelia Shepherd, 2010–present)

CAMILLA LUDDINGTON
(Dr. Jo Wilson, 2012–present)

JERRIKA HINTON
(Dr. Stephanie Edwards, 2012–2017)

TESSA FERRER
(Dr. Leah Murphy, 2012–2014, 2017)

GAIUS CHARLES
(Dr. Shane Ross, 2012–2014)

KELLY McCREARY
(Dr. Maggie Pierce, 2014–present)

MARTIN HENDERSON
(Dr. Nathan Riggs, 2015–2017)

GIACOMO GIANNIOTTI
(Dr. Andrew DeLuca, 2015–2021)

KATE BURTON
(Dr. Ellis Grey, 2005–present)

STEVEN W. Bailey
(Joe the bartender, 2005–2010)

MOE IRVIN
(Nurse Tyler, 2005–2014)

SARAH UTTERBACK
(Nurse Olivia Harper, 2005–2018)

JOSH BYWATER
(Intern No. 1, 2005)

SENDHIL RAMAMURTHY
(Intern No. 2, 2005)

MONICA KEENA
(Bonnie Crasnoff, 2005–2007)

JOSEPH SIKORA
(Shane Herman, 2005)

SUNKRISH BALA
(Steve Murphy, 2005)

JEFFREY DEAN MORGAN
(Denny Duquette, 2006–2009)

KALI ROCHA
(Dr. Sydney Heron, 2006–2007)

CHRIS O'DONNELL
(Dr. Finn Dandridge, 2006)

EMBETH DAVIDTZ
(Dr. Nancy Shepherd, 2006–2019)

KYLE CHANDLER
(Dylan Young, 2006–2007)

FAITH PRINCE
(Sonya Cowlman, 2006)

MARK SAUL
(Dr. Steve Mostow, 2007–2012)

MERRIN DUNGEY
(Dr. Naomi Bennett, 2007)

AUDRA MCDONALD
(Dr. Naomi Bennett, 2007–2012)

PAUL ADELSTEIN
(Dr. Cooper Freedman, 2007–2013)

LAUREN STAMILE
(Nurse Rose, 2007–2008)

MADISON LEISLE
(Lisa, 2007)

JAMES IMMEKUS
(Andrew Langston, 2008)

ROBERT BAKER
(Dr. Charles Percy, 2009–2016)

NORA ZEHETNER
(Dr. Reed Adamson, 2009–2010)

SHARON LAWRENCE
(Robbie Stevens, 2009)

SARAH PAULSON
(Dr. Ellis Grey, 2010)

MICHAEL O'NEILL
(Gary Clark, 2010)

ART CHUDABALA
(Jerry Adams, 2010)

TINA MAJORINO
(Dr. Heather Brooks, 2012–2013)

JUSTIN BRUENING
(Matthew Taylor, 2013–2018)

HILARIE BURTON
(Dr. Lauren Boswell, 2013)

REBECCA FIELD
(Sabine McNeil, 2014)

GEENA DAVIS
(Dr. Nicole Herman, 2014–2018)

SAMANTHA SLOYAN
(Dr. Penelope Blake, 2015–2016)

MIKE MCCOLL
(Dr. Paul Castello, 2015–2019)

SAVANNAH PAIGE Rae
(Winnie, 2015)

JAICY ELLIOT
(Dr. Taryn Helm, 2017–present)

Sophia Ali
(Dr. Dahlia Qadri, 2017–2019)

Matthew Morrison
(Dr. Paul Stadler, 2017–2018)

Alex Landi
(Dr. Nico Kim, 2018–present)

Amy Acker
(Dr. Kathleen Shepherd, 2019)

Beanie Feldstein
(Tess Anderson, 2020)

Rob Lowe
(considered for Dr. Derek Shepherd, 2005)

The Writers

Shonda Rhimes
(2005–present)

Krista Vernoff
(2005–present)

Stacy McKee
(2005–2018)

Tony Phelan
(2005–2014)

Joan Rater
(2005–2014)

Mark Wilding
(2005–2012)

Harry Werksman
(2005–2007)

ERIC BUCHMAN
(2005–2007)

JAMES PARRIOTT
(2005–2007, 2015)

CAROLINA PAIZ
(2006)

JENNA BANS
(2008–2012)

JEANNINE RENSHAW
(2011–2014)

ELISABETH R. Finch
(2014–present)

The Directors/Producers

ZOANNE CLACK
(2005–present)

ROB CORN
(2005–2017)

PETER HORTON
(2005–2007)

JEFF MELMAN
(2005–2007)

MARK TINKER
(2005–2008)

BILL D'ELIA
(2009–2019)

DEBBIE ALLEN
(2010–present)

ROB HARDY
(2013–2015)

The Production Staff

NORMAN LEAVITT
(makeup artist, 2005–2018)

MARTY CARRILLO
(electrician, 2005–2007)

MIMI MELGAARD
(costumes, 2006–2018)

TOM BURMAN
(special effects makeup, 2006–2018)

MATT MANIA
(key grip, 2006–2012)

NICOLE RUBIO
(script supervisor/paramedic Nicole 2007–2017)

The Musical Artists

ISAAC SLADE and JOE KING of the Fray

GARY LIGHTBODY of Snow Patrol

INGRID MICHAELSON

The ABC Executives

STEPHEN MCPHERSON
(ABC Entertainment Group president, 2004–2010)

CHANNING DUNGEY
(ABC Entertainment Group president, 2016–2018)

The Staff of *Entertainment Weekly*

HENRY GOLDBLATT
(editor in chief, 2002–2019)

JENNIFER ARMSTRONG
(senior writer, 2002–2011)

MICHAEL AUSIELLO
(columnist, 2008–2011)

MELISSA MAERZ
(senior writer, 2011–2016)

RICHARD MALTZ
(photo editor, 1994–2017)

NICHOLAS FONSECA
(senior editor, 1999–2009)

MARK HARRIS
(executive editor/columnist, 1989–2010)

Reporters Who Cover *Grey's Anatomy*

KRISTIN DOS SANTOS
(columnist/on-air TV expert, E! Entertainment,
2001–present)

LESLEY GOLDBERG
(West Coast TV editor, *The Hollywood Reporter*,
2003–present)

I remember I was on a plane with Isaiah Washington, T. R. Knight, Jim Pickens, and Patrick Dempsey, headed to Seattle. It was during the third season of *Grey's Anatomy*, when we were definitely at the height of our popularity. We were walking through the airport. Of course, nobody knows me because I'm the writer. But it was like being with the Beatles. People would stop them every thirty seconds to get a picture.

We mostly shot in the woods, which was an hour's drive outside the city, but we also shot on the streets of Seattle. That was crazy, because women were on their way to work and would just stop because they were all of a sudden face-to-face with the *Grey's Anatomy* actors. Anywhere from three hundred to four hundred people would gather, just to watch. The actors were very gracious and posed for pictures. But, seriously, I even said to somebody, "Where are you supposed to be?" And she said, "Oh, I was supposed to be at work forty-five minutes ago, but I'm not gonna miss this."

It was definitely a fun time to be in television.

—Mark Wilding, former executive producer
for *Grey's Anatomy*, 2005–2012

HOW TO
SAVE A LIFE

CHAPTER 1

"Pick Me, Choose Me, Love Me,"
Or, How It All Began

S ome of the best shows in television history came from un-remarkable beginnings. Test audiences notoriously loathed the 1989 pilot for *Seinfeld*. *CSI* was one of the last pilot scripts in 2002 to be ordered by CBS, which had far more faith in its remake of *The Fugitive*, starring Tim Daly. And then there was *Grey's Anatomy*, a 2005 midseason replacement for *Boston Legal* that was written by a TV novice whose biggest credit was penning *The Princess Diaries 2: Royal Engagement*. The stakes were relatively low for Shonda Rhimes and her drama about five randy interns working in a Seattle hospital. ABC wasn't in immediate need of another water-cooler drama, having just launched *Desperate Housewives* and *Lost*. And the last network to create a must-see medical show was NBC in 1994, when *ER* gave us a McDreamy in George Clooney before we even knew we wanted one. And yet the audaciously confident Rhimes, a USC film school grad and self-described addict of surgery shows, was convinced she had something special on her hands.

Shonda Rhimes (Creator) I always associated hospitals with good things. That's where I got fixed. We all think of doctors as amazing and magical, but they're just people at work.

Stephen McPherson (Former ABC Entertainment Group President) Shonda had done a pilot about female war correspondents that everyone loved, but it was not something we were interested in. We were really encouraged by Shonda's writing. We thought the television industry was due for a medical drama.

Peter Horton (Executive Producer) It was always about the relationships. It was primarily a story about Derek and Meredith, and longing. You saw these two people and how they longed for each other.

Ellen Pompeo (Dr. Meredith Grey) I thought it was about five interns and [Meredith's] mother.

Peter Horton Derek and Meredith were the cornerstone of that show. The opening scene of the piece is the two of them having just slept together in a one-night stand. Now, it was like, "We can't be together because you're my boss." That becomes the obstacle that the two of them have to negotiate with and dance around for, you know, years.

Stacy McKee (Writer) The original script was really long, an unmakeable draft, ultimately. We ended up shooting quite a bit of it, but obviously you can't have a three-hour first episode, so you have to cut a lot out and shift some things. At one time Preston Burke and Richard Webber may have been related. There were a few relationships that might have shifted over time. But the core story was always there.

ABC didn't look far for its star intern. Pompeo, a former L'Oréal model who broke out in Brad Silberling's 2002 comedy, Moonlight Mile, *was already roaming the halls of ABC after starring in the network's failed TV pilot called* Secret Service.

Ellen Pompeo The network didn't go for it. Me . . . as the head of the Secret Service!

Shonda Rhimes I kept saying, "We need a girl like the girl from *Moonlight Mile*!" Finally somebody said, "I think that girl is Ellen Pompeo. We have a deal with her at ABC."

Ellen Pompeo I said, "I hate medical shows! They make me think I'm gonna die all the time." And they said, "Please just go meet Shonda." So we had lunch at Barney Greengrass in Beverly Hills, and after I met her it was like, "I want to do this show." I just liked her. We were the same age. This may sound weird, but she's a Black woman, and I always really feel comfortable around Black people. I married a Black man! And I trusted her. She had a vision for the show.

Peter Horton She's got that "every girl" beauty. She's not model-y, she's not overtly gorgeous, she's just beautiful. That's exactly what Meredith needed to have.

Ellen Pompeo To come from where I come from, no entertainment background, not even having the slightest idea how to get into show business? I just felt so blessed to be making a living this way.

Katherine Heigl had a little more experience than Pompeo, but not by much. Also a former model, she appeared in Under Siege 2: Dark Territory *before costarring as Isabel Evans in The WB's* Roswell *for three seasons. For her* Grey's Anatomy *audition, Heigl tried to look smart by wearing a sweater and glasses and putting her hair up in a bun. She even considered dyeing her hair brunette to "trick" Rhimes and Horton into thinking she could play a doctor.*

Peter Horton Trying to find someone that beautiful who really *can* act is really hard. It's like trying to find a guy in his forties to be a lead in a series these days, with all of the competition out there. Katie came in and just nailed it. There were a couple other girls we were considering, but Katie just obliterated it.

Stacy McKee She was wearing glasses in the pilot. I think her hair was probably up in a bun for the pilot, as well. We lost the glasses pretty quickly, though, because it was sort of a nightmare with the reflections, and glasses are hard to shoot. You'll note there are a number of scenes, even in the pilot, where she's wearing them for a split second and then puts them on top of her head really quickly so they wouldn't reflect all of the lighting.

The execs weren't initially looking at stage actress Chandra Wilson to play the role of the cranky Dr. Miranda Bailey.

Instead, they targeted Sandra Oh, a Canadian-born actress who'd appeared in HBO's Arliss *and opposite Diane Lane (and future* Grey's *costar Kate Walsh) in the 2003 film* Under the Tuscan Sun.

Sandra Oh (Dr. Cristina Yang) I was wearing a pair of scrub pants and had my hair in pigtails. I came in and read for Shonda, her producing partner Betsy Beers, and Peter Horton. And it was great. And then they came back and said, "We want you to read for Bailey." And I was at that point in my personal space where I wanted to ask for what I wanted, and I didn't want to play Bailey. I said, "What else is available?" And they said, "Cristina is available." For me, at that time, I was interested in playing a role that was the antagonist. In the pilot, she was the antagonist and also not in a position of authority. Bailey had authority; she was their teacher.

Peter Horton We said, "Sure." She went away for a little bit, studied the sides, came back, and read for Cristina. She was brilliant. And right about that time, we got this tape from out of nowhere from New York of Chandra Wilson reading Bailey. We were like, "Oh, my God. That's Bailey and Cristina, no doubt about it."

Harry Werksman (Writer) We called Bailey a Nazi [in the pilot]. If you were to meet Chandra herself, she's the sweetest woman, the antithesis of what you see on-screen. It's remarkable. Anything on *Grey's* was always done to take the piss out of it. There was no evil connotation with calling her a Nazi. It's just [meant to call her a] taskmaster. It's much catchier to call someone "the Nazi" than "the taskmaster."

Jenna Bans (Writer) Shonda was always really aware of being inclusive. But I also remember that she didn't want to sacrifice a joke, in a good way. And sometimes for comedy, you can't be so worried about offending. You're going to offend someone. So she had a really good sense of sort of walking that line of not wanting to say anything that she didn't believe in as a person, but also, you know, being true to the characters. And sometimes people are a little offensive and say the things they shouldn't. She kind of let us have free rein with that type of thing.

Chandra Wilson (Dr. Miranda Bailey) People leave me alone because they think I'm mean. I'm not mean . . . I'm misunderstood.

Tony Phelan (Writer) Shonda managed to fill that pilot up with people who had a lot of stage experience, probably more collectively than they did experience in TV. But that meant they were really well-trained actors.

That described James Pickens, Jr., who had trained at the Roundabout Theatre in New York before taking recurring roles on Curb Your Enthusiasm *and* The West Wing. *He was cast as Dr. Richard Webber. And T. R. Knight had appeared on Broadway in* Noises Off *before making his TV debut opposite Nathan Lane in the short-lived TV series* Charlie Lawrence.

Peter Horton T. R. Knight just did a great read for George. He just came in and was so unique, his rhythms and his intonations and everything, they're just unlike anybody else. We'd seen so many people come in and play that part really shy, embarrassed, and, you know, self-deprecating, and he came into it with all of that, but with a kind of a determination of, "But I'm going to be as good as any of these people." That grated into his quirkiness. T.R. being T.R. just made him stand out.

T. R. Knight (Dr. George O'Malley) Who was I coming in? [Casting director] Linda Lowy really stuck her neck out, and I was so appreciative of that.

There was even some discussion about whether George should be the show's only gay man.

Harry Werksman There was certainly a desire to include a gay character on the show. We eventually got it [first] with Callie, but she was bisexual. I do remember having some discussions about it and about a gay character and looking over the cast at the time. George seemed to make sense. Alex was the macho guy, and it clearly was not McDreamy or Burke. We were like, "Well, it could be George." We had no idea that T.R. was gay. So we talked about it, but I think we were just like, "Eh, if it works in a story [we'll do it]." I think a pin was put in it. I think that was about as far as it got.

The daughter of Hollywood royalty Richard Burton was re-cruited to play the pivotal role of Meredith's mom, Ellis, a world-famous surgeon whose brilliant career was cut short because of Alzheimer's disease.

Kate Burton (Dr. Ellis Grey) I was forty-six years old and I was looking at television stuff to do. I got a call from my manager, who said, "There's the part of the mother of the lead-ing lady who's a surgeon, but now she's in a nursing home and has early-onset Alzheimer's." And I literally thought, Are you kidding me? Ellen [who was in her thirties at the time] was ob-viously too old to be my child.

Finding Burke and McDreamy took a bit more doing. Paul Adelstein was cast in the role of Dr. Preston Burke, but the actor had to drop out due to conflicts with shooting the movie Be Cool. *(Adelstein would later rejoin the Shondaverse as Dr. Cooper Freedman, Oceanside Wellness's pediatrician, in the* Grey's Anatomy *spin-off* Private Practice.*)*

Paul Adelstein Shonda is very strong at writing to the actors she has, so I think my Burke would have been a completely different animal.

Isaiah Washington (Dr. Preston Burke) I didn't audition for Burke, I auditioned for McDreamy. I had a beard and Afro and was going for a Ben Carson character at the time. Shonda and I thought it was a great idea to represent a brain surgeon who looked like Dr. Ben Carson. That didn't go that way. There's a rumor out there or something that Ellen didn't want me to be her love interest because she had a Black boyfriend. The context is that she's not into white men. I guess she im-plied that her boyfriend may have had a problem with her doing love scenes with me, so she felt uncomfortable. I sup-ported her with that.

Peter Horton The network wanted us to cast Rob Lowe as Derek Shepherd. He's not exactly who we had in mind for

McDreamy, but we met with Rob. He had a choice of either doing our show or *Dr. Vegas* for CBS. He chose *Dr. Vegas*. Then we
were like, "What about Patrick Dempsey?" At that point, Patrick
kind of already had his career and no one was really paying attention to him. The network initially was resistant to it, but we
really felt right about it.

Tony Phelan Rob Lowe! That pilot could have gone in a
very different direction.

Rob Lowe (Actor) My picker was awesome! The real, honest
reason was [former CBS Corporation chairman] Les Moonves's
pitch to me. His personal pitch was amazing, and there was no
pitch from ABC. ABC just never said anything. I just had a better meeting with CBS. The scripts were incomparable. The vibe
around *Dr. Vegas* was great. The script for *Grey's Anatomy* was
great. I went with the vibe over the script. The rest, as they say, is
McDreamy.

Patrick Dempsey (Dr. Derek Shepherd) I needed something that let me play a leading man with edge. People had
such a strong idea of who I was, based on who I had played
years ago. I was so over it.

Ellen Pompeo I definitely was involved in the process of
hiring Patrick. Ultimately I don't have a say; the network is going to do what they want to do. But they saw the chemistry
between us. There were five or six guys in the final process, and
I read with all five of them. And then I think they only brought
three or four to the network. And then they watched the audition, and it was quite obvious right off the bat that Patrick and
I had the best chemistry.

Patrick Dempsey With Ellen, there was the magic. I just

played with her. We were just present to each other and listening to each other. It was always very magical, but very professional.

Shonda Rhimes We called him Dr. McScreamMeFuckMe during the pilot. [McDreamy was] the PG-rated version. It's really amazing that this thing that we came up with while shooting the pilot, just because Patrick Dempsey is so adorable, stuck.

An additional four actors—Josh Bywater, Sean Palmer, Grinnell Morris, and Sendhil Ramamurthy—were cast as background interns who might have gone on to become characters in their own right. But they never made it past episode one. (Ramamurthy was later cast as geneticist Mohinder Suresh in the NBC sci-fi drama Heroes.) *Two other bit players from the pilot, however, got to stay in Seattle for a long time.*

Josh Bywater (Intern No. 1) That made me feel really good about myself, because I was not Intern Number Two or Intern Number Three. It was an under-five role, which is an actor who has under five lines. I said something about Izzie being a supermodel. I can vaguely recollect some notion of wondering if this might grow into something bigger. I don't think at the time anybody knew really what was going to happen.

Sendhil Ramamurthy (Intern No. 2) I had gone in and read for T. R. Knight's part. Shonda really liked what I was doing but said, physically, I just didn't look like how the character should look. She was like, "We love you, would you do Intern Number

Two in the pilot just like a consolation prize?" Five lines? I'll take it. It was either my first or second job on U.S. prime-time TV since I left drama school.

Moe Irvin (Nurse Tyler) I remember seeing Gabrielle Union in the waiting room for my callback. I thought I did a good job. I didn't hear anything for about three weeks. Then I got a call that said, "We're casting you as Tyler." Apparently there was kind of like a juggling thing between me and Steven Bailey. I'm thinking he was considered to play Tyler at one point, but they cast him as Joe and me as Tyler. I likened my role to a good meal that you're preparing: you need a little bit of spice to kick it up. That's what Tyler was. Tyler would come in, throw a jab here and there, spice things up a little bit, and then I was out. I wasn't trying to come in and throw a bunch of crazy shit like, "Look at me."

Steven W. Bailey (Joe the bartender) I actually auditioned for the role of the guy who died in the pilot. George promised he was going to be okay and then he died. I read for that and they offered it to me, but unfortunately I wasn't able to do it because I had something that ended up not going over at Fox. A lot of people don't realize this, but I actually played a different role for a few episodes in season one. I played an anesthesiologist, believe it or not, with a couple of little lines of, like, "Pressure is dropping," or, "I'm pushing some kind of medication," or whatever. I think they had plans to develop that character, and then somewhere along the line they decided he wasn't a thing they wanted to do, and so they came up with this Joe guy instead.

Filming on the pilot began quietly at an abandoned veterans hospital in Northridge, California.

Peter Horton We needed a practical hospital that had the topography that could double for Seattle. Since I was from Seattle, I was being really picky. When we walked into the lobby of Northridge and looked out that huge lobby window, I could've sworn I was looking across Lake Washington to Bellevue! The fact that it's a veterans hospital was an added bonus in that it was almost empty, sadly. Perfect to shoot in.

Stacy McKee There were a lot of empty buildings. Our writers' offices were literally hospital rooms. The windows were nailed shut because, apparently, it had been a psych ward or something. We were pretty sure it was haunted and it was just kind of this bizarre, weird bubble that forced everyone to bond really quickly. Everything was right there, so it really added to the sense of camaraderie, not just with the cast but with the crew. It was pretty special.

Eric Buchman (Writer) ABC basically treated the show as if it were a low priority. They had two shows with lead characters named Dr. Shepherd. *Lost* also had a Dr. Shephard! At no point did anyone get the note saying, "Maybe you should consider a different name since you'll both be on the network." It seemed to me like no one cared.

Josh Bywater It was the first big set I'd ever been on. T.R. was great. We were shooting a scene in the cafeteria and he's supposed to be eating because he's nervous. He just kept eating. The more takes we did, he said, "I need a bucket. What am I doing to myself?" And I grew up watching Patrick Dempsey in

Can't Buy Me Love! He came in and said, "Hey, I'm Patrick." I'm all, "I fucking know who you are."

Stacy McKee Patrick walked in with a certain sense of knowledge, like he understood what was happening a little bit more than some of the people who hadn't done a lot of projects prior. He was so gracious. I remember the first read-through. There was a catered lunch or something. I just remember sitting at a table with food and him walking around and shaking hands with most everyone who was in the room and introducing himself. It was really nice.

Patrick Dempsey I've been around long enough that my hopes weren't up too high.

Moe Irvin I remember Jon Voight came on the set. He was godfather to Skyler Shaye, who was the first patient in the pilot. I remember going, "What the fuck, man? This shit is real. These people ain't playing around." I had done one other pilot, commercials, stuff like that. But not to this level.

Once Rhimes and Horton found their perfect hospital, special care was taken to make sure the doctors looked authentic but not too hot.

Mimi Melgaard (Costume Designer) At the very beginning, Shonda wanted the scrubs to look real, but real scrubs are totally ill fitting. They're huge. We altered them all, but we wanted them to look real. We didn't want to make them look like they zipped up the back, but we tried to make them as flattering as possible within the reality of the show. The thing that was really challenging as a costume designer for *Grey's* is that everything had to be subdued. The story was first, and the clothes couldn't distract from the story at all. If someone's coming into the hospital, it's emotional. I worked really hard to never have the clothes upstage anything. Even in surgery, you see the bottom of the scrub cap and their eyes. I didn't want anything to distract from their eyes, even in those real tight close-ups. I wanted the character and the story to come out. I don't want someone to go, like, "What coat is that?" Or, "Ooh, that's a cool bag." We never wanted that, so we kind of developed this Seattle look, which was a muted color palette. Also, when the show started, my intention was to have the clothes really subtle. I kept thinking that the show was going to go into syndication, so I wanted the clothes to look timeless.

Norman Leavitt (Makeup Director) Peter Horton wanted everybody to look, like, rough and ready, to try to keep them looking real. They're medical people just taking care of stuff, without makeup. I don't think Shonda or Betsy Beers particularly liked that. They were young, pretty people anyway, what are you going to do? My whole thing was to do no harm. As the episodes went along, I don't know, the network, Shonda, Betsy, whoever else was in there, wanted a little more glamour. It's a TV show.

With everything finally in place, filming began in 2004.

Peter Horton My original opening for the pilot was Ellen lying naked on the couch. The opening scene of the pilot was Derek and Meredith having just slept together in a one-night stand. We had a very tight lens that was out of focus, going over all the curves of her body. You didn't even really know what it was as the credits were rolling. [Her body] would come into focus as her eyes opened. It was this beautiful description of *Grey's Anatomy*. We just didn't have time for it, plus Shonda had an instinct to start the show with more of a bang than the grace of that. I kind of regret it. We seriously could have kept it.

Former ABC Studios Executive There were big debates about the big reveal [of Meredith's romp with Derek]. Most of the men wanted to take the scene out. You're taking your heroine to a place where she's too promiscuous!

Shonda Rhimes I got called into a room with a bunch of people who said, "You can't put a woman on television who had sex with a guy the night before she started work." Because they said no woman does that, and the kind of woman who does is really trashy. There were all these old men in the room, and I had no idea how to respond. The moment I knew that Betsy Beers and I were going to be friends for the rest of our lives, she opened her mouth and said, "I fucked a guy the night before my first day of work." She told the raunchiest story, and none of the men could get away fast enough. And no one ever brought it up again.

Former ABC Studios Executive We did the right thing and listened to them.

That wasn't the only disagreement over the pilot.

Harry Werksman At one point Steve McPherson hated the title *Grey's Anatomy*. So for a week we were called *Complications*.
Eric Buchman That was a book out there called *Complications:*

A Surgeon's Notes on an Imperfect Science. So Shonda said, "Eric, you need to go read this whole book just to make sure that this writer can't accuse us of basically stealing his book." It was written by Atul Gawande. It was a good book, and there were similarities, because they're both about what's it like to be a young doctor working for a hospital for the first time. There were things that would overlap. I heard that ABC went and optioned the book just so they could officially use the title, but I do not know who made the call to go back to *Grey's Anatomy.*

Kate Burton When my manager called me, he said, "They're doing this show called *Surgeons.*" That was the working title.

Eric Buchman I also remember someone in the room pitching—and it might have been me, I hope it wasn't me—somebody pitching the name *Miss Diagnosis.* I'm pretty sure it was a joke. Shonda just outright hated that.

And something—or someone—felt like it was missing from those intern gatherings in the lunchroom.

Former ABC Insider We had three really big pilots that year: *Grey's Anatomy, Lost,* and *Desperate Housewives. Grey's Anatomy* tested better than *Lost* or *Desperate Housewives,* but the concern was that *Grey's* was very generic, very derivative. And the concern was, how do you make a medical drama break out? Steve McPherson also felt, looking at the research, that there was something missing in the characters. They needed to add another younger male character. He wasn't going to schedule the show until he was happy with what the second episode looked like.

Tony Phelan We had shot the whole pilot without Justin

Chambers. One of the notes after the pilot test was: "You need a bad boy. You need a male member of the intern class who's not just an asshole, but male."

Peter Horton So we shot his scenes with him later.

Tony Phelan If you go back and watch the pilot, you can see how they surgically put Justin in everywhere.

Justin Chambers (Dr. Alex Karev) There were definitely nerves. I was with all these other actors, I didn't know anybody, hoping that the show would be a success. Thank God it worked out.

Still, the addition of a new series regular wasn't enough. McPherson continued to have concerns, which did nothing for his reputation.

Stephen McPherson I remember one time, Gary David Goldberg said that the worst executive he had ever worked with was Stephen McPherson on *Spin City*. There's just one small problem with that: I never worked on *Spin City* in any capacity, in any way, at any time. I wasn't even at the network that it was on during its run! I also, to this day, have not ever met Gary David Goldberg.

Peter Horton ABC was very worried. We had this one time where they decided our show wasn't colorful enough. I had a business affairs woman come up to me and say, "Do you think that poster is colorful enough?" I mean, it was really absurd. Steve McPherson was a very controlling executive, more so than any I've ever worked with. We had this locker room scene in the pilot where they're all meeting. It was shot with a steady handheld camera. Steve called us up after he saw those dailies and said to Executive Producer Mark Gordon, "I can't sell this show because you do those shots that aren't steady." I mean, it was like an overreaction to every little thing.

Stephen McPherson Being in the job I was in, you have to very quickly get used to constant pessimism about every single thing you do. But that's the nature of the game.

So he shut down production after the producers turned in the first episode. His reaction was so unforgettable that twelve years later, executive producer/showrunner Krista Vernoff told The Hollywood Reporter: *"He hated it. He said to [then ABC executive] Suzanne Patmore Gibbs at the time, 'This show is going to be the chapter in my book titled "Why I Should Trust Myself or Why I Should Trust People I Hire."'' Because she forced that program on the air. And then it was a great big hit, and he got all the credit."*

James D. Parriott (Co-Showrunner) Steve was surrounded by women he trusted very much and in executive positions, and they told him it was wonderful and our test results were good. We tested four episodes that first season and they all tested very well. So we knew we had something.

Peter Horton ABC was convinced we'd blown it.

Former ABC Studios Executive The rough cut was terrible for the second episode. It wasn't terrible in the sense that it wouldn't work for TV, but it was shot very dark because they were going for a cynical look. You have to light dark-skinned individuals really well when you shoot sixteen millimeter, because otherwise you won't see them. They didn't shoot this particular scene very well, and you couldn't see two of the people.

Harry Werksman Steve was unhappy with a particular scene that had already gone through the approval process. The scene was about one of the terrible jobs that interns are given: having to deliver bad news to patients. Alex and Cristina were given that bummer of an assignment, so they turned it into a contest of who could deliver the bad news the fastest. We made it funny, these two type-A personalities competing with one another.

James D. Parriott One of the stories that we told was about a woman who had been raped and was beaten almost beyond recognition. They find the head of the guy's penis in her stomach. It was really dark but very Shonda-esque. It was a really brilliant episode. And then Karev and Cristina were tasked with giving bad news to people. It was very funny, but it was dark. Steve McPherson, it turns out, had just lost a close friend to cancer and was feeling very sensitive about it. Steve saw that and was outraged.

Harry Werksman Apparently Steve saw it, hated it, and said, "This is not the show. This is not what will go on ABC." So he shut the show down.

James D. Parriott We changed it to where they're running around telling good news and we changed the makeup on the battered woman to be a little less severe. That's all that happened.

Peter Horton We had to have big meetings and I was like, "Okay, I'm going to get fired. Writers are going to get fired. They clearly see something totally different than what we see." They had a big meeting, where all they basically said was, "You have to make sure the show is colorful, happy, uplifting, and positive." And then they fired my director of photography. They blamed it on him, for no reason. Everyone else took a two-week break.

James D. Parriott It was a larger issue. It wasn't just, "Oh, gee, that's too dark, fire him." We felt that he was dismissive and gruff and so that was all part of it, too. The way I've heard some executives present it is like they saved *Grey's* and turned *Grey's* around. We didn't change any of the scripts that we shot before that episode.

Peter Horton Then we started up again and nothing really changed.

Stephen McPherson Shonda and I have joked since then. I guess I was a little foulmouthed while being straight with her about this amazing show. But we had some serious work to do. To her credit, she heard it and did the work, made the changes, and off it went. So to say the person who develops the show, picks up the show . . . it's kind of an odd position to take that I hated the show.

Stacy McKee No one thought it was going to be a phenomenon at that point. We were all just doing our part to make this little thing we all believed in, to give it the best chance of moving forward. It was new to everybody, including Shonda. We all were just hoping and dreaming.

Grey's Anatomy *premiered in the 10:00 P.M. time slot on March 27, 2005, a Sunday night. The reviews were mixed, to say the least. Terry Kelleher of* People *wrote, "To be worthy of study,* Grey's Anatomy *needs more of a brain." The Hollywood Reporter's Barry Garron asked, "Can this medical drama be saved? Not without radical surgery." A second-year surgery student at Mount Sinai Hospital in New York City told EW's Kristen Baldwin, "If I'm really going to respect this show, by the sixth episode I want to see bags under the eyes. I want to see yellow teeth from drinking too much soda on call. I want to see a unibrow on somebody. Still, I think it's a great show." The divergent commentary aside, the premiere episode earned an 11.1 rating among adults eighteen to forty-nine—the equivalent of fourteen million viewers. It was the most-watched midseason drama since the premiere of* Dr. Quinn, Medicine Woman *twelve years prior.*

Patrick Dempsey The pilot was great. And then just the discovery of what was happening . . . I couldn't believe how it came together. And the bands that came on, and the emotional impact the music had on the show. Everybody had great moments. You realize how powerful an ensemble can be, and it was the collective that made it successful, not one individual.

Stephen McPherson Jeff Bader was head of scheduling during my entire tenure and he would call me in the mornings after premieres. I would wake up and work out, usually on a treadmill, and my wife would come in and go, "Jeff's on the phone." I remember when he called me. It was way beyond our hopes. I mean, it just exploded on the air. Truthfully, we didn't have a lot of media money to spend on midseason shows. So, it was mostly on-air promotion. But that is the most effective way. Billboards are more for egos than for selling shows.

James D. Parriott Our pilot numbers came in the first night and they were good but not fantastic. We dropped from *Desperate Housewives*. But then we started hearing things after that first week. Somebody would come in and say, "Hey, I was just at the gas station and these two women, they were filling their car and they were talking about our show," or, "I was in the supermarket and I heard people talking in line."

Kate Burton It had shown on Sunday night for the first time after *Desperate Housewives*. That Monday, I was sitting on the subway in New York doing the crossword puzzle, and this woman standing next to me said, "So are you doing the crossword puzzle to keep the Alzheimer's away, Dr. Grey?" I had only been in one scene! But that scene became one of the indelible scenes in television. I've been to a few Alzheimer's benefits. They often show that scene because it was the first time that a character with Alzheimer's was portrayed on network television.

Tom Burman (Special Effects Makeup) Here's what I told [then producer] Rob Corn after we did the pilot. He said, "What do you think?" And I said, "Well, I don't know who's gonna watch this. It's doctors with teenage dialogue. It's really a soap." I said, "I can't imagine anybody wanting to watch this. I think it's so stupid." He said, "Well, we'll see what happens." So how wrong was I?

Isaiah Washington I think America was ready for diversity, all kinds of ethnicities, because of *Survivor*. People were used to rooting for regular-looking people. That's what I really enjoyed about our cast. Everyone could pick someone, an Asian, a blonde, an African American.

Sarah Utterback (Nurse Olivia Harper) I began shooting the day after the pilot aired. Those huge numbers came in and the excitement on the set was just magnificent. It was like everyone was relieved and excited. Some actors had done three or four or ten pilots that hadn't gotten picked up. This was a hit immediately. I think it really filled everyone up with a lot of confidence and excitement. I'm really grateful I was there to witness that, because it influenced me and revealed what is necessary to make a show work. You have to have that cohesion and common goal among everyone to make the best show possible.

Josh Bywater Ever since then, and I can't believe I'm saying this, I've wondered if I would've been able to make Intern Number One into a bigger part. I like to fancy the idea that I could have been an Alex Karev. We will never know now!

Sendhil Ramamurthy No one has ever walked up to me on the street and said, "I loved you as Intern Number Two from *Grey's Anatomy*." It's always about *Heroes*. But I still get those residual checks for that one little thing in the pilot. Honest to God, I probably made more than ten times in residuals over what my one-day fee was for appearing in the pilot. [His scene often pops up in clip packages whenever a TV program looks back on the *Grey's* pilot.] I met up with the cast at the 2007 Golden Globes. By that time I was on *Heroes*. We had been nominated and *Grey's* had been nominated for Outstanding Drama. I walked by their table kind of sheepishly, because who the hell is going to remember Intern Number Two? They all stopped me to say how happy they were for me. Shonda told me, "Well done." For someone who had like four lines in the pilot and then they hadn't seen me in three years, it was a very cool thing.

Ellen Pompeo The show is not really about me, it's about all of us. Even though my name is in the title, it's not a typical show that way. The show is just as much about everyone else. I think we're all equal. This show works because of everything that comes together. That's what the magic is. It's not any of us by ourselves.

Patrick Dempsey The first episodes were done in a bubble, so we had no idea what we were doing or how it was going to come out. We weren't sure we were going to get picked up, and everybody was freaking out about missing pilot season. "What if we don't get another gig? How are we going to pay the rent?" We wrapped those episodes and it premiered, and literally overnight everything changed. After fifteen years in the business, I had overnight success.

CHAPTER 2

"The Fairy Tale May Be Slightly Different Than You Dreamed," Or, Working with an Ensemble

Those early years of *Grey's Anatomy* were among the most jovial. Though the hours were long and arduous, everyone basked in the show's great ratings and found ways to celebrate their good fortune. Sandra Oh would make margaritas on Friday nights. Ellen Pompeo would pay for food trucks when the craft services chow wasn't up to par for the crew. Eric Dane and James Pickens, Jr., would spend lunch breaks at a back table in the Emerald City Bar playing poker with the key grip and camera operator. Everyone participated in football gambling pools, including guest stars such as Christina Ricci (who actually won). And when the schedule allowed, some of the actors dug up their cleats and mitts for weekend softball games in a local entertainment league.

Patrick Dempsey They let me race, which was remarkable. For the most part, they did a phenomenal job at scheduling and making it possible for me to race as much as I could, which I'm so grateful for.

Matt Mania (Key Grip) I remember very long hours. In fact, the entire time I was there, it was seventy-hour workweeks. I remember a guy asking me, "Why are you guys doing seventy-plus hours a week? Isn't it just a bunch of doctors standing around a bed talking?" I couldn't really answer his question: this guy's got a point. They were concerned about getting a lot of coverage, that was the number one reason. Shonda wanted to cover every scene really comprehensively, and I just don't think they really paid a lot of attention to going long every day. There was not a lot of worrying about overtime.

Nicole Rubio (Script Supervisor/Paramedic Nicole) There were days that started at like two in the afternoon because we had shot so long into the night the day before. We hung in there because we believed in the show. We wanted it to be successful. Nobody was complaining. We were just doing the job.

Patrick Dempsey It's a lot of work for everybody—for the writers, for the crew, anyone who is there every day. We're well compensated and fortunate, but we were doing seventeen-hour days back then.

Sandra Oh So it was extremely satisfying when a large, really diverse audience is enjoying the show.

Mimi Melgaard Since they were working that many hours on a show every single day, everyone really fell in love with the scrubs. It's basically like wearing sweats to work. It didn't matter if you ate pizza last night. It didn't matter if you were cold; you could put your long underwear underneath your scrubs. No one would care.

Steven W. Bailey It was like you were at this really exciting summer camp when you were a kid. I mean, it was just electric. They were all friendly. There was nobody who was standoffish or weird. It just felt like everybody wanted to get to know each other better and work together.

T. R. Knight When we were all together, the amount of fun we would have [was] sometimes a little *too* much fun. We were a ragtag team of weirdos with a kind of unexplainable chemistry.

Kali Rocha (Dr. Sydney Heron) I knew T. R. Knight from my New York City days. He had been in a Broadway show and I was in the replacement cast for the same Broadway show. So we had that connection. We'd always joke around and laugh. And one day I was like, "You know what, I'm going to take you out to dinner." He was so sweet about it, but he totally rebuffed me. And then of course, like two years later, I was like, "Oh, you're gay. Got it, got it." He was a gentleman about it, but clearly it wasn't something he was ready to reveal. He was never, like, "You're gross." He was just, like, "Yeah, no to Tuesday. Um, my dog's getting washed."

Jenna Bans There was always an actor in the [writers'] bungalow. Eric Dane would stop by, Chandra Wilson would stop by, a bunch of them would stop by all the time. They were really cool about showing up for little birthday celebrations. We worked in such close quarters, which is such an amazing thing that you don't get anymore because so many shows are shot out of town. It was a really easy collaboration to have because we were, like, a hundred feet away onstage.

Steven W. Bailey *Grey's Anatomy* has all these big emotional scenes, all these big medical emergencies. So you kind of think working on that show might be intense. I'm sure it was for everybody else, but any day I was working it was like a holiday for everybody because it meant they were in the bar. It meant that they weren't doing medical jargon all day and weren't wearing scrubs all day. They were wearing street clothes. Most of the time you have a six-or seven-day shooting schedule, but only one day in the bar. Everybody's usually pretty happy in the bar. I feel like it was a very relaxed atmosphere most of the time. It seemed like it was their favorite day of the week. I didn't have to experience the stressful part. I would just show up, which would usually be one day an episode or something, and it was always the fun day. I won.

Moe Irvin I remember in those early episodes, we would all just sit around in Sandra's trailer with Ellen and Katie. We were all just kind of chilling.

Matt Mania There were no cliques. Everybody hung out with everybody. Nobody avoided anybody.

Marty Carrillo (Electrician) All I know is that Katherine could smell out food. You'd be working on a Friday night, and our bosses would go out and buy an Indian dinner because sometimes we didn't want to eat catered. She would come right around the corner and smell it and we'd already have a plate for her. And then when Krispy Kreme was coming into town when they were big and hot, she had a Krispy Kremes–eating contest with one of the stand-ins to see who could eat the most. She did. She loves sugar.

Moe Irvin A lot of that didn't happen as the seasons went on. It became, "We're not fucking around anymore," you know what I mean? There was more pressure on those guys. They had to be on their game.

Ellen Pompeo I so [looked] forward to scenes with all my peeps because when everyone [came] in it [was] so much fun. We [had] a great time when we're together. Then I [got] to do my deep emotional stuff with my patients, then I [got] to do my great relationship stuff with Patrick. It's a great way to make a living.

> *Rhimes and Beers recruited a talented and diverse group of writers—many of whom, such as Peter Nowalk* (How to Get Away with Murder), *Marti Noxon* (Girlfriends' Guide to Divorce; Sharp Objects), *Allan Heinberg* (Wonder Woman), *Jenna Bans* (Good Girls), *and Stacy McKee* (Station 19),—*went on to become big successes on their own. Krista Vernoff, who joined the show in its first season, would become Rhimes's most trusted collaborator and end up serving as showrunner in the later seasons.*

Harry Werksman We'd really become a fairly tight-knit group through those first three seasons. ABC was good enough to send the entire writing staff on retreats to Cabo to stay at a beautiful resort, all expenses paid, to start breaking the next season.

Mark Wilding (Writer) We had a real camaraderie. I made

great friendships on that show more than any other one. I still go on ski trips with Tony Phelan, Joan Rater, and Krista Vernoff. It's a great group of folks.

The writers quickly formed strong bonds of their own—but it wasn't over how to mix the perfect margarita. Writing for such a massive ensemble and churning out up to twenty-six episodes a year was a formidable challenge.

Jeannine Renshaw (Writer) My biggest issue in writing for *Grey's Anatomy* was all the characters. It literally seems I couldn't remember, you know, Sandra Oh's character name, because I'm terrible at names.

Tony Phelan You say to yourself, Okay, I've got twelve characters, and we have a large writers' room, and each of these twelve characters needs a three-beat story in every episode. If you look at the structure of the show, the middle of each show had some kind of lunchroom scene where the interns would come together, talk about their individual cases and what was going on in their lives, and then go back to their stories with some kind of adjustments.

Mark Saul (Writer's Assistant/Dr. Steve Mostow) I would help document what was going on [in] the show in what they would call the Bible. It was a very thick binder that was divided up by seasons. It had all the story lines and guest casts and just everything you needed to know, so that if you were writing something and said, "You know, who was that character who came in two seasons ago?" they would go back and look through it.

Jenna Bans They made me take a quiz. I thought it was a joke, but it wasn't a joke. They wanted to make sure, rightly so, that I had seen all the episodes, which I had. This went on for, like, a couple of weeks. I had to stand up in front of the writers' room, and the questions were hilarious and insane, and it was sort of half a joke, but I was sweating. I was the only one in the history of *Grey's Anatomy* who had to take that quiz.

Tina Majorino (Dr. Heather Brooks) At first, for me, it was a little bit overwhelming because of how many people are in that cast. Normally when you step onto a show it's only a few people you have to get acquainted with, but there were days where twelve or more actors were there. It's a totally different atmosphere because of that. On those bigger days, it was organized chaos for sure.

Carolina Paiz (Writer) Really what you're dealing with is probably six story lines because people break down into pairs, whether it's friendships or romances. And then because you do have the three medical stories, three of those stories sort of blend into that. It'd be like, "Okay, this is a Burtina [Burke and Cristina] story line."

Stacy McKee It was super fun because it's like solving a puzzle. You have all these characters you need to service, season-long stories you want to service, and individual stories for just the episode you want to service. And then everything was anchored by a theme and you throw some medical in there. We were all learning about the medical as we went along.

Harry Werksman One thing Shonda said early on is that the medical cases are mirrors that are held up and the patients and their medical cases are mirrors for the doctors to look into and see their own journey.

Kevin McKidd (Dr. Owen Hunt) What is most beautiful about our show is that while some stories are fluffy and silly and just purely there for entertainment, sometimes they are about something important, too.

Jenna Bans When you're dealing with a medical show, there's a handful of things that are likely to happen, which is dying, getting fired, and getting your license taken away. So we definitely cycled through those.

Sarah Drew (Dr. April Kepner) I remember Shonda calling me right before I read the episode where I got fired. She called me to assure me that I wasn't going anywhere, so I was like, "Oh, thank you for telling me before I showed up at the table read and thought, Am I done here?" I was fired and rehired twice on the show.

Patrick Dempsey You never [knew] where you [were] going to go. It [kept] evolving. It [was] constantly in flux and very organically [kept] changing, so you never [knew what was] happening. For me, it was an exercise in just being present and focusing on, What am I doing today? Learn the lines, be in the moment, and go from there.

Rhimes was brilliant and instinctive, but she was still an untested showrunner. To assuage the network's fears about handing over the kingdom to a novice, ABC brought in veteran TV producer James D. Parriott (Dark Skies; Push, Nevada) to keep the train on the tracks. But the show was

Rhimes's vision, so everyone ultimately deferred to her, Parriott included.

Shonda Rhimes I'm a shy person by nature, and suddenly I have a job in which I'm required to communicate with twelve actors and an entire crew and a studio network and writers.

James D. Parriott I came in while it was still called *Untitled Shonda Rhimes Project.* We definitely comanaged. She was learning the first season and second season. I mean, she's brilliant, absolutely brilliant, and by the second season she was running the show completely. She was very, very precocious, a quick learner. But yeah, the first season anybody who starts [off for the first time] needs somebody who's done it a million times before, and I had done it a million times before. So, yeah, she had my help.

Nicole Rubio It was figuratively and literally her show, but he would come in as support . . . a very strong voice in the room. And on set, he would come down. But a lot of people didn't even know that Jim Parriott was there.

Eric Buchman He made sure that he wanted the writers to work decent-enough hours that they could go off and, like, live their life and have stories to come back in. So the room hours were like 10:00 A.M. to 6:00 P.M. that first season.

James D. Parriott We became Mom and Dad in the writers' room.

If there was ever a time the writers adored Rhimes the most, it's when she was forced to go toe-to-toe with the network's

standards and practices department. S&P was there to make
sure nothing crossed the line and raised the ire of sensitive
viewers, who would sometimes retaliate by notifying the Fed-
eral Communications Commission. But if you're making a
show about doctors, somebody at some point is going to have
to say "penis" and "vagina"—whether S&P liked it or not.

Stacy McKee I wish that there was a collection somewhere
of all the exchanges between broadcast standards and practices
and Shonda. They were awesome and hilarious and just amazing.

Jenna Bans Shonda Rhimes was the most fun person to
watch have those arguments. It was kind of my favorite part
of the job, and I've totally sort of tried to emulate her as I've
moved on to running my own shows. She was so smart in the
way she would argue with them. There was something in one
of my episodes where a piece of medical equipment looked
phallic. They were worried about the equipment looking like
a penis. Shonda was like, "That is a legitimate piece of medical
equipment." I can't remember what it did, but she was like,
"The fact that we can't show something that surgeons use all
across this country because you guys think it looks like a penis
is insane." They finally backed down.

James D. Parriott That episode where they pulled the penis
out of the woman's stomach? We went through about twelve
versions of blurring it before they would approve it. That was in
the days of more severe broadcast standards, for sure.

Jeannine Renshaw I remember the episode "I Bet It Stung."
A guy gets stung by basically masturbating with a hornet's nest.

That's the one where we wrote "penis" too many times. S&P wrote, "I wanted to touch base with you regarding the penis mentions. Obviously it's fine to say 'penis,' but it would be helpful if we could reduce the current ten penis references by a few so they don't start to sound crude and gratuitous." It was so earnest.

Stacy McKee There was a conversation between Callie and Meredith at the bar. They were talking and using the word "vagina" in basic conversation, maybe three times. I think it was even medically based. A note came back saying, "You can only use 'vagina' once." I was, like, "What?" These are doctors, and they're using the anatomically correct terminology for body parts that they actually *have*. I respectfully declined it, and then what ended up happening is Sara Ramirez wound up saying the word "vagina" probably twenty times. Many vaginas made it into the cut.

Mark Wilding I think Bailey was pregnant, and for some reason T. R. Knight's character was helping her deliver the baby or something. That was the one where she said something like, "Don't look at my vagina," or something. We had done two or three episodes in a row where we mentioned the word "penis." All of a sudden [S&P] were like, "You can't say the word 'vagina.'" Shonda was like, "Give me a break. That's ridiculous. What's the matter with you people?" That's when we came up with "va-jay-jay," to skirt S&P.

Harry Werksman That came about once Addison was introduced as being a neonatal OB-GYN. Of course she's going to call that part of the body what it's called.

Tony Phelan This assistant on the show, Blythe Robe, was maybe twenty-three, twenty-four. Shonda was like, "Okay, young people, do any of you have any euphemisms for your lady parts?" And Blythe was like, "Well, my friends and I call it a va-jay-jay." Shonda said, "Great! From now on, it's a va-jay-jay."

Mark Wilding It was funny because S&P couldn't really say anything about it because it wasn't "vagina." But of course, it sounds way dirtier than "vagina."

Shonda Rhimes When I turned on the morning shows the day after the Super Bowl episode and everyone was using the word "va-jay-jay," that was really surreal.

Jenna Bans I remember there was a sex scene between Callie and McSteamy and the note was, "We see too much side flank on one of them." They were worried we saw a little too much of the side of one leg. And not the thigh, not even the groin region, but *the side* of one of their legs. It was always kind of this absurd push-pull. Shonda was always really aggressive in a good way about fighting back and really protecting what makes the show special and fun.

Tony Phelan There was never really anything that we felt that we wanted to do but couldn't. One of the things that stood out for me and Joan Rater was when we made the decision that Cristina was going to get an abortion. Of course, this was a huge thing and everybody was very concerned about it. We said, "We're going to build this. We're not going to do it as a one-off, we're going to build her arc this season toward getting her to that decision. It's going to be a hard decision, but if we do our job right, it's going to be a decision that the audience, even if they don't agree with her, they at least will understand why she made the decision." We got, like, no hate mail. There were no protests, there was no nothing. It was just another episode.

Table reads were the high point for everyone. It was exciting for the writers to hear their words performed by the actors, and the stars were equally enthusiastic to learn what fresh drama Rhimes and her staff had in store for the doctors of Seattle Grace. But, as if on cue, someone always walked away from the table wanting more.

Nicole Rubio Everybody was excited to be there, enthusiasm all around. The scripts were a bit funnier back then. They laughed over T.R.'s character, the way they wrote for him. He was always a joy to watch. And Chandra Wilson! There was always a release of something you could chuckle about and then you got into the major surgeries, something you could cry about.

Harry Werksman As a producer on the show and on any show, really, there is always drama, there's always turmoil, there's always someone who is not happy with their lines.

Carolina Paiz I certainly remember there being a lot of tension. After every table read, the actors would line up outside Shonda's office. I know there was a lot of back-and-forth.

James D. Parriott She would say, "Okay, now I'm going to be in my office. Who wants to talk to me?" The actors raised their hands and she would go to Ellen first, then Patrick. She would take all their questions. She wanted no crap on the set. They had the argument and then she'd put out the final script and that was it. They all respected her for that.

Eric Buchman Basically, we wanted to avoid situations

where the cast is asking [a writer] to change the script on set. Because the idea was that once those cameras start rolling, you shoot what's on the page.

Mark Wilding I think Shonda was really pretty tough about stories and dialogue and that sort of stuff. If you were an actor and you wanted to rewrite something, you had to go through a lot of hurdles.

Jeannine Renshaw I think that it's the nature of the business that you try to be collaborative and you try to listen to their feelings, but it's also sort of like being a parent: This is my limit. You have to say this line.

Mark Wilding There were times when they wouldn't say lines or whatever, and I would get annoyed. We had this old guy named Charlie, who was a patient in a coma, and the interns used to have lunch in his room. I wrote the episode where he woke up and then he wanted to die because he didn't want to live anymore. At one point, all the interns gathered around his bed and he died by then, so it was an empty bed. T.R. put a chocolate bar down on the bed. I was watching from video village and said, "What the hell is that? What is he doing?" I asked the set decorator where he got it and he said, "Well, he wanted a chocolate bar." I said, "There's no chocolate bar in the scene!" I go up to T.R. and ask, "What are you doing?" T.R. goes, "I think Charlie and I both like chocolate." I'm like, "You've never talked about liking chocolate. There's never been any kind of chocolate bond established. You cannot put a chocolate bar on that bed."

Jeannine Renshaw Sometimes you'd have seven people in a scene. You learned to try to keep the scenes as small as you can, but sometimes you'd have the staff meetings. I remember one time Jesse Williams, God bless him, didn't feel like he had anything to do, so he wanted to be on his cell phone texting. This was before Instagram and everything, so people weren't on their phones as much. He felt like it would give his character something to do. And I was like, "Jesse, it just looks like you're not interested because you're on your phone. Act like you're interested in what's happening."

Complicating matters for everyone was the show's extreme growing pains. The situation was different in the first season: all nine episodes were completed before the pilot even aired, and there was still a prevailing feeling at the network that it wouldn't go the distance. Once Grey's *became a hit, the pressure was instantaneous. "At the time, it was just a real combination of exhaustion and stress and drama," Pompeo told* Variety *in October 2020. "Actors competing with each other . . . and envious." While ABC boosted the episode orders, Rhimes and her writers were trying to service a large ensemble of actors who were suddenly a huge source of fascination in the press and in public.*

Patrick Dempsey The energy would change when I went into a room. It was like, "Oh, they're talking about me." It was wild. Wild. It's crazy, because you go from trying to get in a room to audition, to suddenly everybody in the world knowing you, no matter where you go. And it happened within a thirty-day period. I'm glad I had the experience to handle it, because it's very heady.

Peter Horton There was consequently an air of tension, but also excitement, because we were breaking new ground. Discovering the show as we went. Pushing boundaries. Seeing how good we could be.

Harry Werksman From the writer/production side of it, we were dealing with any number of issues. We were still struggling against that burden of satisfying the president of the network and delivering stories and scripts that we were happy with, the stories we wanted to tell, but at the same time weren't pushing the buttons that were gonna have him cancel us at the next stage. We learned as we went along, and as writers we're also like, "Yeah, maybe you don't wanna do that. That's gonna require twenty people in the OR and take eight hours. Let's find another surgery to do." We all learned, and it was just a learning curve.

Moe Irvin There was more pressure on those actors, their dialogue. You've got to learn to say what they tell you, walking and talking with all that medical dialogue. That's a motherfucker, man. You gotta be skilled. You gotta be on your game.

Eric Buchman The stories got more complicated and more characters joined the cast and keeping track of all those characters with three medical stories and all their personal lives was a lot. The writers' room hours eventually got worse as it became harder just to keep track of everything.

Tony Phelan At times we were doing, like, high twenties in episodes. It's very easy to get burned out, and it's very easy to just feel like you're, you know, on this endless hamster wheel.

Harry Werksman The window between when a script gets finished and when it's shot got smaller and smaller and smaller.

Stephen McPherson After the Super Bowl [in February 2006], they were household names, and it all changed. There was a lot of drama that didn't need to be there. A lot of it is well documented, and it's always unfortunate. These successful shows, they're few and far between. And to see them get caught up in that kind of meshuggaas? Everybody was being paid a lot of money. They became famous at the craft that they chose. It was unfortunate.

Matt Mania We spent a lot of time waiting for actors to show up on set. Early on, the actors probably took control of that agenda and never gave it up.

Harry Werksman I'm sure as an actor, if I were an actor and I'm sitting in my trailer, I'm like, "Goddamn, my call time was eight and it's eleven and I haven't shot anything yet. What the hell?" I understand that. Nobody wants their time wasted.

Matt Mania Nobody early on put their foot down as far as the hours were concerned from the production side. It just became, that's what it was. That was how it was going to be.

James D. Parriott I don't think the change in the actors really happened until seasons three and four. When you're servicing that many characters, it's very hard to get all the characters to have big story lines in every episode. And they all began to resent Shonda.

CHAPTER 3

"You Give Them Someone to Run To," Or, the Care and Feeding of Fans and Media

Shonda Rhimes sensed early on that engaging the fans was paramount to her success, so she created a show blog and required her writers to contribute. But there was a downside to launching such a forum: fans felt obliged to share their strong—and sometimes negative—opinions. It only got more aggressive when Rhimes, as well as her stars, began using social media. Then the floodgates opened.

Ellen Pompeo Not everyone's going to like you. I don't like everybody that I see on TV, you know what I mean? You can't set out to try to have the whole world love you. I mean, that's just like a weird ego thing. I'm not amazing and perfect and great. I always expect people aren't going to like me.

Jeannine Renshaw We'd get letters about every single character. There were people who hated Cristina at first, and then they loved her. I don't think anybody ever hated Meredith. She was pretty generally loved.

Harry Werksman I had written an episode right around the time of the Super Bowl when the Seattle Seahawks were playing the Pittsburgh Steelers. I'm a huge Pittsburgh Steelers fan, so I went to the party and sat in a room with Steve Bailey— Joe the bartender—and watched the game while everybody else was out enjoying a party. My blog post was about how Joe the bartender and I sat and watched the game. A sort of behind the scenes, right? I got so many angry responses from fan blogs saying, "Who cares about football? Who cares about what you did at this party? What about the episode?" Lesson learned. My blogs after that were all about what happened in the episode and what Meredith was feeling. The blog was instant access, whether we liked it or not. Fans, which is short for fanatics, of shows really begin to feel like they own the characters. Sometimes as writers we were like, "Yeah, we're glad you watch and we're glad you love the characters, but they're not yours." There's a real possession that people take, particularly of long-running shows and particularly with shows that have such amazing characters and relationships.

Tony Phelan If somebody died or something happened or somebody got married, whatever, you would have fans who would say, "I hate this. You have ruined the show and I am never going to watch again." And then that name would go away, and then six months later, you get another "I hate this.

You've ruined the show." The name would be different, but the IP address would be the same.

Gaius Charles (Dr. Shane Ross) I learned quickly how intense *Grey's* fans are.

Brooke Smith (Dr. Erica Hahn) There was an entire page devoted to my bad teeth. I was like, Oh, man, I gotta get Invisalign, which I did! So, there you go. I prefer having straight teeth, so I'm happy for the fans. But these forums! I know a lot of people did not like Hahn, so I think I sort of stopped looking at them, because I thought, This is not helping me. People have a hard time with characters who aren't likable, which is weird to me because I think you need that. Otherwise, where's the conflict? I don't get it. How can everyone be likable? It doesn't make sense.

Sarah Utterback There is no filter, you know? People feel very free to tear people down for very strange reasons. Who knows why? I decided to not look at those because they were not nice. It's the same with a review. It's not really informing the work. The work comes from the writing. That's my job. My job isn't to be likable.

Sarah Drew The first probably three seasons I was despised. April at first was a pretty grating character. She was written that way. I had another nail in the coffin by having a crush on McDreamy, so of course everybody was angry at me for trying to get in the middle of the show's most important relationship. There was a lot of hate actually spewed at me.

Nora Zehetner (Dr. Reed Adamson) Oh, they hated Reed. She was very headstrong and feisty and obviously butted heads with a lot of the regular characters that people had grown to love, so I think I knew from before [my first episode] even aired that I was not going to be anybody's favorite character. Still to this day, I get tagged on Instagram with how much people hate Reed with, like, a picture of me lying dead in a pool of blood.

Robert Baker (Dr. Charles Percy) It was pretty negative. People have for years not been able to separate reality from fantasy, and my character was no exception. I'm from Memphis and I was in a bar with my younger brother and a friend of ours, and there was this group of young ladies. One of them came up—I'm assuming she was a little drunk—and punched me right in the shoulder. She was like, "You got Izzie fired!" It's laughable now, but I didn't find it very funny at the time.

Lauren Stamile (Nurse Rose) One day, I got on a message board. *That* was a mistake. It was tough, because it was kind of in the middle of my run. Years later, I can take that with a grain of salt. But I was pretty upset by it. People were very spirited in their words. And if you're in the middle of working on something and you're letting other people's experiences impact what you're doing, that can really hurt the storytelling.

Tessa Ferrer (Dr. Leah Murphy) I think originally fans didn't like how inept my character was. Not only was she not really good at what she was trying to do, she was also a little bit of a nitwit. Then it was the nail in the coffin when she and Arizona started having a little fling.

Samantha Sloyan (Dr. Penelope Blake) When people remember me, you can kind of see it on their face. They're like, "Oh, I remember what you did." It's this thing with *Grey's*

Anatomy. You have to learn to love these characters that are created for you. I am just so grateful to be a part of that world. I told no one [that I would be in Derek's death episode], so everybody was just tuning in to watch and was startled by what happened, to say the least. Some of my very old friends made it clear they were upset with me. They still loved me, but it was going to take them a second.

Krista Vernoff (Showrunner) We abhor change, and yet change is what keeps us tuning in every week. I watched *Friends* in my twenties, and every week we would watch, scream, and go, "Oh, God, why aren't Ross and Rachel together? Oh, they broke up again! Oh, God, he married somebody else!" But we didn't go online and make ourselves a caucus to petition the show writers to give Ross and Rachel their happily forever after, or say, "You don't love me." Or, "You must hate your fans." Or, "Why don't you do this for us?" We didn't do that because it wasn't an option. As a television writer, you can appreciate the fans, and you can appreciate their passion. But you cannot listen to them, because if you do, you're lost. If you listen to them, everyone will be happy forever after, there will be no conflict, and there will be no series.

Ellen Pompeo If there are no fans, there is no advertising money. And if there is no advertising money, there is no show. The fans are the show.

But fans could also be generous with their support of the cast. In addition to rewarding Grey's Anatomy *with terrific ratings—the series has consistently remained one of ABC's top five most-watched shows since its first season—viewers were always looking for up-front-and-personal ways to express their gratitude.*

James Pickens, Jr. (Dr. Richard Webber) I dig the fans. Different actors have different takes on fans and what fans require of them, but I think it's a privilege that we've impacted their lives to such an extent that they have been willing to take this journey. They've been die-hard and they've been resolute in the stories that we have told. They've been with these characters when they've been good, when they've been bad, when they've been ugly, when they've been heroic.

Chandra Wilson When folks come up to you these days, they come up because they just really want to say, "Thank you." They want to say, "I appreciate the journey of your characters." Even the young ones of today who started with Netflix. It's not invasive. It's not crazy. It's absolute appreciation, and I have nothing but appreciation to give back.

Ellen Pompeo Bless their hearts, they are adorable. It's incredible how this show just keeps resonating with the young generation. It's really touching.

Mimi Melgaard They would come to the studio gate, or Patrick Dempsey would have a special guest, or someone won something. Or they were from Children's Hospital. Everyone was energized by their passion. It felt so good to give back to someone in person, because we don't [usually] have that connection. We're always behind the camera. I think the actors get it, but then when we see people who are such passionate fans, we're like, "Wow, you love it, cool. Come on in."

James Pickens, Jr. They find out where we are [when we shoot in Seattle]. Production says, "Don't tweet anything, don't Instagram anything until we get back." But they find out.

Chandra Wilson That's our joy for going up there, to actually get to play in the place that we've been talking about. So, yeah, they would find us and hang out.

Brooke Smith It's so funny because I was buying a mattress the other day, and I kind of bonded with this older couple in Sherman Oaks. We were like, "Oh my God, we're not leaving this store until we get a mattress!" Then all of a sudden the guy said, "Oh my God, you gave that [leaf] speech!" I have a big giant book that a bunch of fans sent me telling me their stories. They all sent leaves. It was very sweet.

Robert Baker It's funny, if I go anywhere in the middle of the country, somebody recognizes me. It's amazing how it stays around. Now it's younger people, teenagers, coming up to me. It's a real testament to how that show has done. I died in the sixth season. It's been ten years and still, probably once a month if not more, somebody comes up to me.

Kelly McCreary (Dr. Maggie Pierce) I frequently get asked, "Have you performed enough surgeries at this point where you feel like you might know what to do?" The answer to that is, "I could cut you!"

Jessica Capshaw (Dr. Arizona Robbins) I got a call saying that [my son] wasn't feeling well, so I rushed to the school. I walked in and the nurse looks at me and goes, "Oh, I get it." And I said, "I'm sorry, what?" And she says, "Your son said his mom was a doctor."

Tina Majorino Now that I'm on social media, I still get

messages to this day from people saying they miss Mousey, which is of course very, very heartwarming for me.

Harry Werksman I teach writing at the American Film Institute. One of the things I tell my students is that audiences will know more about characters than they probably will know about their best friends. You see them at their happiest, their saddest, their angriest, whatever the emotion is. People react and identify with that.

Kali Rocha Mainly when people recognize me, they're like, "Oh, you're that crazy girl!" A few women have sort of been, like, "You went on a date with McDreamy?" They want to know what Patrick was like. And he was just lovely. I mean, he's a total husband and father. Like, he was just totally lovely on set.

Moe Irvin I never even thought people were paying attention to my character. I just kind of came in and wanted to be a team player. I wasn't trying to do anything flashy, so I didn't think anybody was paying attention to me. But I remember one time I was doing a play over on Melrose Avenue and I was on a break so I went to get coffee at Starbucks. I walked across the street and a woman stopped in the middle of the street as I crossed, jumped out of her car, and was like, "I love your character!" Apparently they were paying attention! After I was gone, I started to see things in the trades like, "Tyler was one of the best nurses on the show and one of the most missed people on the show." Who knew?

Jerrika Hinton (Dr. Stephanie Edwards) There's a strong fan base of people who really miss Stephanie, and I appreciate them.

Steven W. Bailey I have this weird, very self-centered theory about why my character was popular, and it has nothing to do with my performance. I feel like Joe was an advocate for the audience. He didn't work in the hospital, he wasn't the doctors we were following. He was somebody who was observing the doctors, just like the audience. I feel like subconsciously . . . I don't know, maybe that's a bunch of bunk, but I can't figure out otherwise why he seemed to resonate so strongly. I really only had three or four episodes that I was featured in—you know, adopting the children, the camping trip, those sorts of things. Most of the other stuff was me just going, "Here's your beer," and saying a snarky remark.

Sarah Drew and Jessica Capshaw were treated to an unexpected display of gratitude after it was announced that they would be written off the show in 2018. Drew was already busying herself on a new pilot for CBS, which was an update of the classic CBS drama Cagney & Lacey, *when she was told to get back to the Prospect Studios lot ASAP.*

Sarah Drew This girl had reached out over Twitter to Jessica. She was like, "We want to do this thing for you guys and we want to make sure you're both there." She was a fan of ours who'd actually been to the set and visited a couple months before. Her dad won a set visit at an auction and brought her on the set. She's such a huge fan of Japril. Jesse Williams and I hung out with her and took a bunch of pictures with her. She's so sweet and lovely and basically rallied the whole thing. She did a GoFundMe campaign and fans raised the money to hire a plane to fly a banner.

The banner that flew over the Prospect Studios lot read: we
♥ sarah drew & jessica capshaw.

Sarah Drew It was so amazing. There were so many amazing things that happened in those few weeks that warm my
heart and I will never take for granted, that I will still hold so
dear for the rest of my life.

Tessa Ferrer *Grey's Anatomy* fans are the most die-hard,
loyal, incredible people. I wasn't a massive character and I
still get stopped in public. People say to my face, whether
it's true or not, "I loved you." I'm surprised that people even
remember me.

*Oh, they do. Fans not only know more of the show's my-
thology than the actors—something that Pompeo routinely
acknowledges on her Twitter feed—they're hungry for any
and all information about the Seattle Grace staff. Oprah
Winfrey tried to take advantage of the fan fascination early
on by taping an episode of her talk show from the set. Meanwhile, several consumer outlets—*Entertainment Weekly
included—turned Grey's Anatomy *into a full-time beat.*

Ellen Pompeo When I got invited on *Oprah* I thought,
Whoa, okay, this is big. I [felt] really lucky. All of us realized
how difficult it [was] to get the stars to align.

Michael Ausiello (Former *EW* Columnist) *Grey's* did mon-
strous traffic right out of the gate, so getting a scoop on the
show just made sense, business-wise.

Henry Goldblatt (Former *EW* Editor in Chief) It was such a water-cooler show. It was important for *Entertainment Weekly* to be in the middle of the conversation.

Jennifer Armstrong (Former *EW* Senior Writer) Soon it felt like I was flying out to L.A. from New York constantly because this show was so huge. I was there so much that at one point, Patrick said something to me like, "I have nothing more to say! How can you have more questions?"

> *Maybe because Rhimes wasn't always so forthcoming. It was nearly impossible to wrestle anything out of the notoriously shy showrunner, who tried to keep a tight lid on spoilers early on by circulating a memo about the danger of loose lips getting pink slips, and posting fake stories on the walls of the writers' room. She was completely guarded when giving interviews, much to the frustration of entertainment journalists. In her 2015 book,* Year of Yes, *Rhimes admits that "when I first got a publicist, I told him and his team that my main reason for having a publicist was so that I never ever had to do any publicity. Everyone thought this was a joke. I was not joking."*

Stacy McKee She was *very* guarded early on. She was new to this whole process, too. Once a couple of things did leak it was like, "If I talk to anybody about anything ever, it's going to come back to bite me. It's better if I just don't." I just think she was worried that she might unintentionally say too much.

Shonda Rhimes I [was] the person demanding that my actors [didn't] reveal anything. We [had] fake stories up on the wall in the writers' room for that very reason.

Jennifer Armstrong Shonda was nice and funny and smart, but it was similar to Ellen in that I think they all understood what was happening and that it was huge. Then it becomes, "Let's not fuck this up by saying something wrong to a reporter." I do remember that this was really the height of spoiler-mania, too. Everyone wanted to know what was going to happen on that show, and Shonda was very much not interested in giving any of that up. I felt like she was always annoyed when we were asking about that. I can't remember if she actually said this or just implied it, but it felt like she was particularly mystified by people constantly wanting to know what was going to happen in this fictional world that came from her own head.

Eric Buchman It wasn't just Shonda. Everyone was bothered by our work being spoiled. And so from that point forward we took it very seriously. What was interesting was that was also before the show was a hit. Like that was just, you know, Shonda just wanting to be respectful. However big our audience was, we wanted to be sure that they enjoyed it.

Stephen McPherson We were making appointment television. We wanted to keep our [big reveals] under wraps for as long as we could.

Stacy McKee At one point there were paparazzi that had made it onto the lot and were camping out, taking pictures. It was a little startling.

Eric Buchman Leaks were a big deal in season one. I forget which site—it's probably not even around anymore—but you would see these spoilers for upcoming episodes and the big one that really upset everybody was when it said, "Oh, Dr. Shepherd's wife is going to show up in this episode." The fact that he was married was spoiled ahead of time! The good news is that the show was not on enough people's radar, so it wasn't ruined for the audience. But it was out there on this one site, and Shonda pulled me into her office and was like, "We need to figure out where they're getting this information from and put a stop to it."

Kristin Dos Santos (E! Entertainment Columnist) When *Grey's* premiered in 2005, I had a spoiler column called "Watch with Kristin" and had been reporting on shows like *Lost* and *Desperate Housewives*, thanks to sources who had access to all the ABC scripts. *Grey's* was a slow burn initially, but by the end of season one, we started seeing significant traffic spikes for *Grey's* spoilers. Somewhere in the middle of season one, I remember revealing that Derek had an "ex-wife," which turned out to be a major spoiler, since Addison introducing herself as Derek's "wife" was the major season-ending cliff-hanger. Soon after, a producer I worked closely with on another show told me that Shonda had called him asking for advice on how to deal with spoilers and specifically . . . me. It was then that I learned the art of the "supertease" and how to keep our audience fully engaged without giving everything away. The next huge thing, Denny's death, went unspoiled. I had a source who had access to every single full episode for many years, and it was always a delicate dance.

Jenna Bans I remember this really funny period of time where [then *TVGuide.com* columnist] Michael Ausiello had a spoilers blog, and he was getting really accurate information to the point where we were all paranoid. We were like, "Wait, how does he know this stuff about characters coming up on the show?" Like, for a month or two we were like, "This man has

bugged the writers' room!" Was someone talking to him? But
we all knew each other really well, and we knew that we would
never [leak information]. We finally realized that he was getting
it from casting breakdowns that were sent all around the city.
So he got it in a totally innocent way.

Michael Ausiello I was still trying to make a name for myself at *TVGuide.com* when *Grey's* premiered in 2005, so trying
to get any official scoop out of the show, be it in the form of
exclusive castings or clips or access to the cast and producers,
was challenging, to put it mildly. So I put all my energy into
cultivating sources. I also remember being extremely competitive with *E! Online*'s Kristin Dos Santos, who was killing it with
the *Grey's* spoilers.

Kristin Dos Santos Covering *Grey's* in the early days was
pure joy and adrenaline. The original cast was a blast on set, despite their later issues. It was the peak era of TV spoilers, when
fans watched each episode live and couldn't *wait* to find out
what would happen next. Ausiello was relatively new to the
spoiler scene, and we became fiercely competitive, constantly
trying to one-up each other and playfully dubbing each other
"best frenemies." That period of time was a lot of fun.

Eric Buchman Different casting agents had a big security
vulnerability where anyone could read all the sides [from the
show on a casting website]. It's supposed to be a password-only
type thing and it was very easy to get around. So we did two
things. First, we stopped using that service entirely. And sec-
ondly, anytime a guest part needed to be cast, I had to take the
sides and change them so that there are no actual details that
give away future spoilers. And not just the big stuff. Even what

medical cases we were doing. So if somebody was supposed to [play a character] with a broken foot, I had to change it to a broken hand. No detail was too small.

Stacy McKee Sometimes we were even tasked with writing fake sides to put out there and throw people off. Scripts were locked down and we just had to be really, really careful with everything.

Matt Mania We were always aware that the show was getting a lot of press, and all of the soap opera aspects of it. Other than causing us overtime because we would wait on one person or another, that kind of stuff didn't really affect us. We were on the front lines when arguments would break out from time to time. You can hear a pin drop when something breaks out like that. You just kind of hang out, wait for it to be over, and quietly start work again.

Patrick Dempsey There [was] a lot of drama in the show. People love gossip. It was unfortunate being in it, but with success comes scrutiny. If things happen, it's going to be talked about.

CHAPTER 4

"He's Gone. I'm Free," Or, How Isaiah Washington Brought Shame to Seattle Grace

saiah Washington's interpretation of the stoic and fearless Preston Burke was a master class in TV acting. The Texas-born actor—who had built a sizable résumé of film and TV roles before joining *Grey's Anatomy*—was both unpredictable and likable, extremely intimidating and sexy as hell. It's no wonder that in 2006, the then forty-two-year-old actor was named one of *People's* 50 Most Beautiful People. Behind the scenes, Washington was considered a generous colleague who was a pleasure to be around.

Harry Werksman He brought real intensity to the character of Burke. He did a lot of research on what it means to be a cardiothoracic surgeon and what a cardiothoracic surgeon goes through.

He very much inhabited that role. There's an old joke: Up in heaven, there are people standing in line for lunch in a cafeteria and the doors burst open and the person goes right to the front of the line and grabs his food. And everyone's like, "Oh, is that God?" And they're like, "No, that's a surgeon." He embodied that.

Eric Buchman The one actor no one ever tensed up around was Isaiah. He would look at his script and he was so respectful of the work. He would circle the punctuation, make sure he got the punctuation correct.

Brooke Smith I remember Isaiah saying, "I'd been told that you were a powerhouse, so I really prepared for your arrival." That was funny. I liked Isaiah. I didn't have any problems with him. I thought he was a great actor.

Nicole Rubio I could watch him for hours. He was well prepared, a delight to have on set.

Marty Carrillo Isaiah loved the crew. He never got mad. He was great with us. The actors all have their own thing with themselves and, you know, we all just sit back and watch and let them go off and do their thing. We just sit there and laugh and go, "Come on, we're already in the tenth, thirteenth hour. Are you going to still go on about it?"

Rob Corn (Executive Producer) From a director's standpoint, Isaiah was always professional. He, like Sandra, was always looking to make things better.

Carolina Paiz He and Sandra had such a grasp on who their characters were. I remember their characters got into a fight in my episode. At the end of the episode, they were supposed to go into the elevator and say something to each other and then hold hands. They were like, "I don't think we need to say anything." They just kind of looked at each other and held hands. I was like, "Nope, you're right. You don't need to say *anything.*"

Shonda Rhimes They were one of the most riveting relationships I have ever seen on television. They were iconic for a lot of people, and Burke was a different kind of Black man than had been seen on television before, and Cristina was a different kind of woman than had been seen on television before. I think that people really loved them together, as damaging as that relationship was for both of them.

But something may have been boiling under the surface for Washington. The show's long hours and frenetic pace were constantly at odds with his professionalism.

Source Close to Washington At least early on, it was not well organized or well run. On a lot of shows a showrunner would say, "Okay, you've got two scenes; come in the morning and we'll get your scenes out of the way so you can go." But Isaiah would sit there all day. Everyone would sit around in their trailers going crazy. You're sitting around bored. You can't really take a nap because you've got to be fresh because someone can come in and say, "Hey, you're on now!" You can't be, like, half asleep. That had a lot to do with what went down on the set.

Kate Burton Everything went a little bit haywire behind the camera. I wasn't in every episode, so it was a little bit like returning to high school and you're like the older teacher. I'd be like, "How's everybody doing?" I tried to just listen and nod my head. Of course, it was very interesting, and some very interesting things came out of it in terms of how you talk to people, what are appropriate things to say, and what are inappropriate things to say.

Case in point: In the late hours of October 9, 2006, Washington was growing impatient on set because Dempsey was late to arrive for a scene that was taking place in Meredith's house. When he finally did show up, Washington lost his temper.

Eric Buchman Whatever happened between him and Patrick, that was not something that I think anyone in the writers' room ever sensed was in the works.

James D. Parriott One of the reasons why the meltdown happened was that it was a night shoot. Everybody was tired and wanted to go home.

Mark Wilding It was my episode. I think one of them had been late to set one day and the other one then decided to pay him back by being late himself. Then it sort of exploded. They got into an arguing match, and then before you know it they were physically fighting. I was standing there in video village. I'm, like, six feet four inches. I'm bigger than both of them. But I didn't really jump in right away because I'm like, I don't know if I want to get involved.

Harry Werksman Patrick Dempsey would show up exactly the moment he was due on set. One of his favorite lines was, "Livin' the dream. Let's shoot this." Isaiah had been there early. He was always there earlier than he needed to be. That was part of his process. And Isaiah, for whatever reason that day, just took that the wrong way and he went after Patrick. I guess he felt disrespected that he and the crew had been waiting. He went after Patrick, pushed him up against the wall, and said, "You can't talk to me the way you talk to that little faggot T.R."

Marty Carrillo I was behind the set and I heard the scuffle going on. I heard, "You son of a bitch!" And then the f-word. Everyone knew T.R. was gay. For some reason, Isaiah just lost it and pinned Patrick up against the wall. You could see Isaiah's pupils go wide, like, "What did I do?" It was quiet. Everyone had to leave the set.

Mark Wilding Katie Heigl did jump in, so did Jim Pickens, and broke them up. Words were exchanged. I remember talking to my wife and saying, "We just had this crazy fight on set, but I think it's all fine now." Everybody went to Shonda's office and worked things out. People yell, that's for sure, but actual physical stuff is very rare. I'd never seen that before. On the other hand, you're also family. You're there for twelve, fourteen hours a day. People are people. Things are gonna explode occasionally. Also, when you're doing twenty-four episodes of TV a year, occasionally tempers flare and nerves get frayed.

Harry Werksman We found out almost immediately what was going on because people were coming over to the writers' office and being, like, "Oh my God, you won't believe what's happened."

Tony Phelan The advantage of having the soundstage right next to the writers' room is that you can walk back and forth. That was really convenient and allowed us to be all on the same team in terms of knowing what was going on and trying to address issues as they came up.

Harry Werksman People retreated to their trailers, so that was pretty much the end of that day. We all felt horrible for T.R. because he had not come out to his family at that point. That was the way the news got delivered, and there was a feeling like, "Oh my God, I can't imagine a worse way for that news to get to your family."

Mark Wilding I didn't think it was going to leak to the press at all, because the fight happened in Meredith's house. There weren't extras around. If it had been in the hospital setting, there would've been extras around, and who knows then? Extras can run to a tabloid and get paid, I don't know, $2,000 for the story. In this case, I think there was somebody in the *Grey's* production office who was secretly working for the tabloids, and that's how it got out.

Source Close to Washington I think it had less to do with homophobia and more to do with his own intimidating nature. It was more about his personality than it was about any homophobia or perceived homophobia. Isaiah was always the first to tell you that he played a gay guy in a Spike Lee movie. He certainly could be a butthead and aggressive, but I don't think the guy was homophobic, truly.

Harry Werksman ABC took it fairly seriously. A day or two later, the entire cast, crew, and writers' room had to do sensitivity training and a course on sexual harassment.

Carolina Paiz I think that was one of the reasons that it was decided we needed producer-level people on set. Because, you know, there was a lot of tension.

Ten days after the fracas, T. R. Knight disclosed to People *that he is gay: "I'd like to quiet any unnecessary rumors that may be out there. I hope the fact that I'm gay isn't the most interesting part of me." A week later, Washington issued an apology, also to* People: *"I sincerely regret my actions and the unfortunate use of words during the recent on-set argument. Both are beneath my personal standards. I have nothing but respect for my coworkers and have apologized personally to everyone involved." Meanwhile, rumors began to circulate that Rhimes would fire Washington and replace him with former* ER *star Eriq La Salle. "I found [those rumors] not only ridiculous but offensive, that we would consider replacing a member of our family," Rhimes told* People. *"The [idea] that one Black man was interchangeable with another seemed disturbing to me."*

Isaiah Washington We learned that we [had] to watch what we say. We [had] to make sure we [were] more accountable.

Patrick Dempsey I think the explosion really healed the show. No one passed the buck, and everyone owned up to the situation and moved on.

Eric Buchman There was this initial incident and things got downplayed. It seemed to almost resolve itself, because my impression was that the issues among the cast were never as bad as things were initially played out to be. What ultimately sealed the fate for Isaiah was when things came up again.

At the 2007 Golden Globe Awards three months later, Grey's
Anatomy took the prize for Best Television Series—Drama.
That was the first time the cast had appeared in front of the
press since the fight between Washington and Dempsey, so
reporters lodged questions about the incident and its antigay
slur. Initially, Washington discussed it by revealing that he
had advocated for making Burke come out as gay, as a result
of the fight: "I love gay. I wanted to be gay. Please let me
be gay." But after the awards show, the question came up
again, and Washington moved to the microphone and de-
clared, "No, I did not call T.R. a faggot. Never happened."
After the party, Heigl, speaking to Access Hollywood, *said,*
"I'm going to be really honest right now, he needs to just not
speak in public. Period. . . . I'm not okay with it."

Katherine Heigl (Dr. Izzie Stevens) I didn't have a coura-
geous moment. I had a couple of glasses of champagne, and I
was furious and frustrated for my friend and sick of the whole
mess of it.

T. R. Knight I was floored. How often is someone going to
stick their neck out publicly for someone, at the risk of getting
slapped in some way, shape, or form? That doesn't happen! But
she's fierce and honest and a great friend.

Michael Ausiello I was in the pressroom and I knew Isaiah
said something incendiary, but it wasn't until later that I knew
he dropped the f-bomb again. I ran into T.R. later that night at
the *Vanity Fair* party and I asked him how he was doing and he
just shrugged. I felt bad for him.

Katherine Heigl I was recently talking to T.R. about this and I said, "I hope I didn't embarrass you and draw more attention to something that you just wanted to go away." And he said I could never have embarrassed him and that he was so grateful because no one had ever stood up for him that way before. So that is a proud moment for me. I don't regret it. And I'm just grateful that my friend doesn't regret it.

ABC immediately did damage control by releasing a statement: "We dealt with the original situation in October, and thought the issue resolved. Therefore, we are greatly dismayed that Mr. Washington chose to use such inappropriate language at the Golden Globes, language that he himself deemed 'unfortunate' in his previous public apology." Washington apologized again and even met with members of GLAAD: "I know the power of words, especially those that demean. I realize that by using one filled with disrespect I have hurt more than T.R. and my colleagues. With one word, I've hurt everyone who has struggled for the respect so many of us take for granted." He even went on to win an NAACP Image Award for Outstanding Actor in a Drama Series. "The first time I was up here I felt deserving of something," he told the crowd. "This time, I feel privileged." The feeling was short-lived.

Harry Werksman It's like, Okay, he's got to go. He's gone. The train had left the station at that point.

Isaiah Washington I did everything that the producers and the network asked me to do. I came back under great stress, and thought I was doing the job I was hired to do. I thought that was going to speak for my future at *Grey's*, but apparently that wasn't the same vision that the network and studio had for me.

Stephen McPherson I feel like it was a mutual decision by the network, studio, and Shonda [to fire him]. Once the facts were confirmed, it wasn't a difficult decision. I don't think we thought it would take down the show, but we did think, God, it's shooting yourself in the foot. You never want to see that happen with any of your shows, with any of your actors, or any of your showrunners. We just thought, Man, this is drama that didn't need to exist and it's unfortunate. He's a really talented actor.

Eric Buchman Fans have a hard time distinguishing between actors and the characters they play. Once it was perceived that Isaiah was unkind to his coworkers—once you have that perception that he might have certain biases or prejudices—it becomes hard for fans to want to root for that character. The one episode that my name was credited on ended with Burke proposing to Cristina. That story line works only if you actually like the Burke character. So as an aspiring writer getting his first big break, [the first time] his first name [is] on-screen, I was very annoyed that real life was making that story line less enjoyable.

Harry Werksman It was a big hole to fill for sure. It's hard when one of your big doctors on the show does something like that and they have to disappear and now you're left with, "Okay . . . what do we do?" But that was the job. We just had to keep going.

Washington's final episode, titled "Didn't We Almost Have It All?," aired May 17, 2007. Burke leaves Cristina at their

*church when her behavior makes it clear that she's not ready
to tie the knot. After realizing that Burke packed up his trum-
pet and his picture of his grandmother that sat by their bed,
Cristina breaks down in her apartment and begs Meredith to
help cut off her wedding dress. "I'm free," she says through
tears. In an awkward twist, Washington also shot a PSA for
GLAAD at the behest of ABC that aired during the finale.*

Mimi Melgaard That was crazy town. I ordered two wedding dresses, and one was cut. We had a panel in back because
you can't really cut through a wedding dress with a pair of scis-
sors. There's the corset and there's so many things that go into
a wedding dress to hold it up. So we had one rigged with just a
big piece of silk in the back so Ellen could cut through it right
next to the zipper. Oh, the metaphors for that dress. That dress
was everything that Cristina wasn't, and who she was trying to
be for the man she loved. She tried everything. She tried to play
that role for him, and she couldn't do it.

Shonda Rhimes The finale finished the character in a way
that is real.

Patrick Dempsey The whole thing was sad, a tremendous
waste. The character of Burke was exceptional.

Nicole Rubio I enjoyed his presence so much that when
they let him go, I just felt like, Oh my God. Who could ever replace him? Dr. Burke was magical. Can we recover? It happened
in a finale. The next season, I think some viewers may have
stopped watching. But then they loved the show so much that
the ratings stayed consistent. I mean, come on! We survived Dr.
Burke leaving! We didn't think it could be possible.

Isaiah Washington I can apologize only so many times. I can accept only so much responsibility. I just hope people in the industry can understand that it's a horrible misunderstanding, what transpired with our show, and it was blown out of proportion.

Katherine Heigl Isaiah thanked me, which I didn't understand. He was almost grateful. He [took] his work seriously and he [loved] his character. He made a big mistake, and it was thoughtless and boneheaded, and I think he's very sorry and embarrassed. This is something that will have changed the scope of his life.

Brooke Smith His departure definitely made way for me. I was never supposed to be told anything until after he was fired. I mean, it just felt weird. I knew he had left already from the media and being in L.A. I just remember I'd gone hiking with my husband and I'd left my phone in the car and when I got back to the phone there were like seventy-five messages. I thought, Oh my God, what's happening? And it was, you know, my manager saying they wanted to make me a regular.

Former ABC Studios Executive He was a fabulous actor. He never got the true credit he deserves. He had his personality issues. I'm not hiding that he's been in unnecessary fights. The gay community never forgave him. But he paid an unnecessarily large penalty for this.

Rhimes, at least, gave him a chance at redemption. To help say goodbye to Sandra Oh in 2014, Rhimes asked Washington to reprise his role one more time in "We Are Never Ever Getting Back Together." In the Rob Corn–directed episode from season ten, Burke offers to bankroll Cristina's research at a hospital he runs in Switzerland. Since he was married with kids, reconciliation wasn't possible, but Cristina wasn't looking for love—just inspiration and a way out of Seattle. Fans, no surprise, were divided in their reaction to the reunion, tweeting screeds like, "Shame on Shonda Rhimes for allowing Isaiah Washington back on Grey's Anatomy," *and, "I'm just so mad that Burke is married now, I thought him and Cristina would get back together," to, "Burke coming back on* Grey's *is almost like if Tupac were to come back to life." Yikes.*

Shonda Rhimes I [had] some people say, "I want them to get back together." I've had some people say, "They can't possibly get back together." I always tell people they need to remember that we're talking about Cristina Yang here. It's not gonna be about whatever you expect it to be about.

Sandra Oh [The scenes were] very energized, as it would be with the person you were about to marry. "I used to look into your face all the time." There were a lot of things to play. He [was a] prepared, energized actor, and he was ready to play. I will say, though, he was nervous.

Jeannine Renshaw It was nice to put a little sparkle, a little tidbit, in there that there was some potential. Who knows? We'll never know if they were going to get back together or not, but just to have something on the emotional side for [Cristina] to look forward to—it was something for us to feel hopeful about.

Shonda Rhimes My first decision and my first responsibility is to the story. I have to be the keeper of the story and make sure that we're telling the story we need to tell, regardless of whatever factors are involved or whatever history is involved. And frankly, Sandra was so lovely and open to do it. It [was] a really kind of amazing experience. I also want to just be clear that Isaiah is a person that we all love and have loved for a very long time. I feel like there have been a lot of people that have been like, "How can you do this?" And I feel very strongly and fully believe in people's ability to grow and change and learn from their mistakes and, when they know better, to do better. If people don't think that over the course of seven years, it's possible for a human being to change, then there really is no future for the human race at all.

Isaiah Washington Dr. Burke [was] probably the greatest challenge I ever had. I studied the medical world extensively. I gave it everything I had.

We'll do it all
Everything
On our own.
We don't need
Anything
Or anyone.
If I lay here
If I just lay here
Would you lie with me and just forget the world?

—"CHASING CARS," SNOW PATROL

Snow Patrol—a Northern Irish–Scottish band made up of members Gary Lightbody, Paul Wilson, Jonny Quinn, and Johnny McDaid—had already completed their fourth album when they got word that *Grey's Anatomy* wanted to use their song "Chasing Cars" for the final moments of "Losing My Religion," the season two finale. The ballad was already the most widely played song of the twenty-first century on U.K. radio. But nobody in America knew how moving the tune was until they heard Lightbody sing about wasting time chasing cars while a distraught Izzie curled up in the arms of her dead boyfriend, Denny. The song—which Sara Ramirez, Kevin McKidd, and Chandra Wilson later covered during the infamous "Song

Beneath the Song" musical episode during season seven—
ended up becoming a shorthand way for fans to express fear
that a sad moment was about to happen on the show.

Gary Lightbody [Lead Singer/Guitarist, Snow Patrol] That
was one of the love songs that I wrote properly. It wasn't a song
about breaking up. It's just a song about being in love. It was
very pure. It was written in 2005; back then I wrote lyrics a
lot quicker than I do now. It was quite a rare occasion that it
all came out at once, you know? All the lyrics came out at the
same time. I was in the county of Kent in England, at our producer Jacknife Lee's house. He has a little studio on the side of
his house and we were writing a whole bunch of songs for the
album, which would become *Eyes Open*. I wrote ten songs that
night, and "Chasing Cars" was one of them. Three bottles of
wine and ten songs. I've never had a night like that again. The
drinking would take over pretty quickly and the writing would
get put to one side, but that night, it worked. Most of the time
I would say, "The best writing comes from a place of trying to
figure something out rather than having something already figured out." I was stable for the first time in a long time. Like, in
that way that was probably a good place to start. It's normally
in the chaos that I write the best, but in that case it was quite
nice to be in the stillness.

"Chasing cars" was a rather crude thing my dad used to say
to me. I didn't have a lot of girlfriends in my early days, shall
we say? I was very inept at that sort of thing. I was very nervous
about asking anybody out, in fact, so nervous I would normally
be paralyzed. So my dad said I was like a dog chasing a car. I
wouldn't know what to do with it when I caught it. He was

right. Chasing cars is really not anything to do with the song, of course, but it's my little nod to him. This was an in-joke between me and my dad.

We got an email from our publisher, who said, "This show wants to use your song, are you okay with them licensing it?" It's all very dotting i's and crossing t's. It's not a romantic thing. It wasn't like a dove came with a letter in its mouth and flew down, which would have been far more appropriate given the scale of what happened. Of course, it was exciting to hear. We'd heard a lot about the show; we were excited to be on it. We just had no idea that it would go the way that it went. Our songs had been on TV shows before: *The O.C.*, *Entourage*, *Smallville*, *Roswell*, there were quite a few. But most of the time, it gives you a day's worth of attention. I guess that's what we were thinking this would do as well. I don't like the idea of music being used to sell something, but if it's to another art form, that's not only fine, it's necessary. Music turns a thing from good to great to life changing.

This is the crazy thing . . . it doesn't happen so much in movies anymore, but it still happens in TV, where a show will be played in America before it gets played in the U.K. or anywhere else. We weren't aware that it had aired. The only thing I knew was when I woke up the next day, it had aired and my phone was essentially melting. There were fifty or sixty messages. We went from outside the top 100 on iTunes to number one overnight. I mean, it was insane. It was already a hit in the U.K., but it wasn't in America.

I'm pretty good at leaving the past where it is in terms of the recording. We do like to mess around with our back catalog in live versions, but as far as the recording goes, I think the song lives where it lives. It's still our most streamed song. It's still getting played on the radio. It's kind of bonkers, the legs that it has, that it's been able to kind of endure for so long. It's just that trying to chase a song like that—excuse my wording—trying to follow up a song like that is never a good idea to try. As I said, it was three bottles of wine in a night. How can you possibly reconstruct a moment of instinct? You'd go mad trying. I've no doubt that somewhere along the line, you know, we'll have a song that'll challenge it. But I'm not gonna try for it, 'cause you'd just go daft.

I did meet Katherine Heigl once. We played at the Greek Theatre soon after [the finale] and some of the cast and crew and writers came and we met them backstage. They were a lovely bunch of people. It was nice that we got to meet everybody from a show that had really done a lot for us. I mean, it really did.

CHAPTER 5

"I Need a Reason to Get Up Every Morning," Or, How Addison Montgomery Kicked off the Spin-offs

B roadcast television thrives on the notion that if a show works, you should make several more versions of it. CBS and NBC have excelled at this shopworn business model: there were a total of six knockoffs of *CSI* and *JAG*, while Dick Wolf spun *Law & Order* off into a multimillion-dollar franchise that launched its eighth spin-off, *Organized Crime*, in April of 2021. As former Carat USA media buyer Shari Anne Brill once told me, "It's less expensive because you already have the writers who are familiar with characters. Since so many new shows fail, the more you can reduce your financial risk, the better off you are." So it wasn't too surprising when ABC opted to create two spin-offs of *Grey's Anatomy*—one in 2007 featuring Kate Walsh's

Addison Montgomery in a new California setting and another in 2017 that would revolve around a Seattle firehouse. Both series were launched as backdoor pilots on *Grey's Anatomy*, and both relied on scribes who'd cut their teeth at Shondaland. But unlike Andy Herrera on *Station 19*, Addison Montgomery had three years to woo fans after she snarled, "And you must be the woman who's been screwing my husband," in the season one finale.

Harry Werksman I wrote that line! Shonda loved it. The nice thing about Shonda is if you wrote it, you produced it. So I was there for Kate's entrance, and what an entrance it was.

Kate Walsh The writers could've made me just hate-able. They did a great job of humanizing Addison.

Eric Buchman That was part of Shonda's original vision of the show. By the time the writers' room was convened [for the pilot], Shonda was already saying, "We're going to build up to [the] episode. We're going to introduce this woman." People forget that the first season was only nine episodes, so it was a very natural thing for us to build the season. We knew it was coming and part of the fun was not tipping our hand, to keep it a surprise. [It was leaked, but] the good news is that the show was not on enough people's radar, so it wasn't ruined for the audience. I truly believe that ninety-nine percent of the audience that tuned in had no idea it was happening.

Unlike other spin-offs that are ginned up in the executive suites, Private Practice *came from the mind of Shonda Rhimes herself. While editing a two-parter for a January 2007 episode of* Grey's Anatomy *in which Addison tells Sloan, "I did want a baby . . . I just didn't want one with you," Rhimes envisioned a new direction for her scarlet-haired beauty. She decided to table a pilot script she was working on about female journalists and pitched the idea of sending her neonatal surgeon to California to Steve McPherson and then head of drama development Suzanne Patmore Gibbs.*

Shonda Rhimes I was trying to figure out a way to complete the character for season three and give her the journey that had been waiting for her.

Stephen McPherson I think I offered to make out with her at one point, I was so happy. There [was] no harm in doing this. Creatively, it [could] stand alone or as a spin-off. There was a huge upside.

For her part, Walsh was still amazed that she had lasted three seasons at Seattle Grace. A relative unknown before she joined Grey's Anatomy—*Walsh's biggest role prior was playing Drew Carey's zaftig ex-wife in his eponymous comedy—Walsh thought she'd be out of Seattle Grace after five episodes.*

Kate Walsh I shot another pilot for ABC. There were always a lot of half-hour shows to do, so I thought, That's probably going to be my life.

Shonda Rhimes The more I spent time with her and the audience got to know her, she became somebody we all really identified with. She looks amazing. She's smart. She has great comedic timing but can also get the big serious moments.

Kate Walsh She told me she wanted to spin off my character, and then I slowly started to leave my body. I was very excited about it, obviously. Totally thrilled! But my first thought
was, Oh, God, what if it doesn't work?

*Initially, Rhimes had hoped to develop the spin-off out of the
spotlight—kind of how she wrote the first script for* Grey's
Anatomy. *But anything* Grey's *related was big news by
then, so news of the idea quickly leaked. Not long after, reports began to surface that Walsh's costars were broadsided
by the news of a spin-off, though execs at the time insisted
that everyone was given a heads-up.*

Tony Phelan I don't think there was any resentment at all
[from the *Grey's Anatomy* actors]. And Kate was, I think, ready
for a new challenge. To have her own show was great for her.

Patrick Dempsey I [was] continually surprised about the
decisions they made. Quite honestly it was an interesting ride,
because no one knew what was happening. It was more of an
issue of them defining what the [spin-off-launching] episode
was about.

Kate Walsh I definitely like writing down goals: where I
want to be, how I imagine it. I didn't write down I'd like my
own spin-off.

On May 3, 2007, ABC aired a two-hour episode of Grey's
Anatomy *called "The Other Side of This Life," which served
as the two-part backdoor pilot for* Private Practice. *It opens
with Addison driving a red convertible to Oceanside Wellness*

Center in California, where she tells her old friend/fellow OB-GYN Naomi Bennett (Merrin Dungey) that she wants to have the baby. The episode also featured Amy Brenneman as psychiatrist Violet Turner, Taye Diggs as internist Sam Bennett, Tim Daly as naturopathic doctor Peter Wilder, Chris Lowell as receptionist William "Dell" Parker, and Paul Adelstein—a former contender for the role of Preston Burke—as pediatrician Cooper Freedman. The two-parter averaged twenty-one million viewers, nearly two million more viewers than Grey's season three average.

Shonda Rhimes I didn't think of it as an all-star ensemble. There's something to the fact that this group is older. Finding a bunch of unknowns at that stage of life felt hard to do.

Tony Phelan *Private Practice* was populated by very seasoned actors, many of whom had their own shows before.

Mark Tinker (Director) I think everyone on that call sheet had been one or two or three on their own show call sheet someplace else. It was a bunch of tremendously experienced and committed actors. That was a fun set.

Kate Walsh It felt like Shonda was peeling off the layers to Addison's tender underbelly. It felt very real to me—taking a trip to see an old friend, and everything just comes out like, "I'm a mess!"

Merrin Dungey The show used the same director of photography from *Grey's* because it was a backdoor pilot and an episode of *Grey's*. So *of course* the look was the same. They used enormous China balls to light us and everyone looked fantastic.

*Two days after the episode aired, Ellen DeGeneres an-
nounced on her talk show that* Private Practice *would be
added to ABC's fall 2007 lineup. But first, some changes
were in order: Dungey would be replaced by Tony winner Audra McDonald, and KaDee Strickland was added as Char-
lotte King, a doctor from a nearby hospital.*

Merrin Dungey I have no idea why I was replaced, but I had
heard that Steve McPherson wasn't a big fan of mine. Working
with Kate Walsh was a lovely experience, and we had a wonderful, easy chemistry from even my first audition with her. She's a
terrific actress to work with and I had a marvelous, albeit brief,
experience with all the cast.

Audra McDonald (Dr. Naomi Bennett) When they were
casting back in February, I was a little upset that I couldn't come
in to audition. There [were] not many three-dimensional African American roles out there in television, so I thought, Everybody's going to want to go out for that.

*After bringing in Marti Noxon to run the writers' room,
Rhimes' goal was to make sure that* Private Practice *felt different from the mother ship. It was so important to Rhimes
that her spin-off didn't feel like "Grey's 2.0" that she sup-
ported the network's decision to air the show on Wednesdays,
not Thursdays behind* Grey's Anatomy. *But the two shows
were still intertwined; crossovers occurred annually, and the
character of Amelia Shepherd (Caterina Scorsone) began on*
Private Practice *before moving full time to* Grey's Anatomy
in season eleven.

Jenna Bans Shonda would sort of go back and forth between the two rooms. But it was a total challenge, because we had all obviously watched *Grey's Anatomy* up until that point. We were starting over with these new characters but still very much wanted to capture Shonda's voice. So it was hard. That first season was really tricky.

Patrick Dempsey She was just trying to keep up with the number of episodes that were demanded of her starting a new show. I think she was feeling overwhelming burnout.

Tony Phelan *Private Practice* was a challenging show because you didn't have surgeries. Shonda wanted to explore this idea of medical ethical dilemmas that the doctors found themselves in. That was the kind of backbone of *Private Practice*. That made it a very different show from *Grey's Anatomy*.

Jenna Bans If you look at the trajectory of that show, we weren't doing surgeries at all. It was set in a private practice in Santa Monica, and there was an internist and there was a cardiologist, and no one but Addison performed surgeries. I remember pitching story lines in that room, and it was hard because a lot of medical story lines that inherently have a lot of drama in them lead to surgery; lead to that life-and-death moment where you're slicing someone open to save their lives. But then we would always say, "Oh, we can't go there." In the later years of that show we ended up going there.

Shonda Rhimes At its core, *Private Practice* felt best when dealing with issues that got everybody in the practice of taking sides. Having strong cases that bring up moral dilemmas [was] important.

Reviews for Rhimes's latest confection were not exactly glow-
ing. EW critic Ken Tucker wrote in 2007 that"the pleasure
to be extracted from Private Practice—*well, not so much*
pleasure as cringey curiosity—resides entirely in trying to fig-
ure out what's really going on inside the actors' heads as they
skip through this latest Adults Are the New Spoiled Brats
fantasy from Grey's Anatomy *creator Shonda Rhimes. I*
look at an intelligent actor such as star Kate Walsh, who
may have figured, 'Hey, spinning my character off Grey's
might be my only shot to lead a TV show, so I'll play along,'
and I wonder how her brain processes such lines as 'I am
the interloper—I don't lope,' which doesn't make sense,
grammatical or dramatic, no matter how valiantly she
parses it." Brian Lowry of Variety *said it "initially qualifies*
as a disappointment—hitting completely familiar medical-
drama beats while pursuing a whimsical tone it never fully
achieves," while Jonathan Storm of The Philadelphia In-
quirer *growled, "It's amazing there's no orthopedist since*
the show's so lame." Still, the show lasted for six seasons and
111 episodes before ABC finally threw in the towel in 2012
(when it was only averaging just over seven million viewers).
The final day of shooting was December 7. The finale, which
aired on January 22, 2013, featured the wedding of Addison
and infertility specialist Jake Reilly (Benjamin Bratt).

Kate Walsh Getting married was kind of awesome. It was
symbolic, sending her off into the world! And all of the cast
was there, so we got to have this massive celebration to end the
series.

Shonda Rhimes Everyone says having two kids is exponentially harder than having one, and it is. Suddenly you have twenty actors and two writing staffs that need your attention. But I don't feel like *Grey's* suffered when my time was spread thin [with *Private Practice*].

It would be seven years before the network approached Rhimes about developing another spin-off. This time, she and Betsy Beers turned to longtime writer/producer Stacy McKee to come up with some ideas.

Stacy McKee It was pretty typical for Shonda's assistant to call and say, "Hey, can you come over and talk to Shonda this afternoon?" We'd go over scripts or whatever. So I packed up my stuff and went over to her office fully expecting notes or something, and it turns out, instead, she wanted to talk to me about doing a spin-off. I really thought she was joking. I was like, "You're messing with me. Shut up, we've got to talk about the episode." But she said, "No, I think the timing is right. So put together some ideas and get back to me." I went home that night and put together probably fifteen ideas, because when Shonda says put together ideas, you put together ideas. So maybe a week later I had a meeting with Betsy to go over my fifteen ideas and the very first one on my list was about a fire station down the street from Grey Sloan. They've dropped off patients at Grey Sloan and there's been this whole world of drama and romance happening under our noses the whole time and we didn't even know. That's basically all I had written down. I pitched that and the opening scene in the pilot. It's the one where they're in the middle of a fire and they put it out and they hear a noise. They move some furniture and see a dog and they stare at the dog for a minute. Then one of the firefighters, Dean, just turns to the other guys and he's like, "There's my puppy." That scene just sort of encapsulated the tone and showed how to turn a firefighter show on its head, innocently. Betsy just looked at me and was like, "We're not reading the rest of the ideas." I wasn't pitching a completely effects-heavy action movie for every episode. That was never my goal or my intention. My intention was to tell amusing character stories in what happens to be a different environment than a hospital.

After casting Jaina Lee Ortiz (Rosewood) *in a leading role as firefighter Andy Herrera, it was decided that Jason George (Ben Warren, a former surgical resident turned paramedic who is married to Bailey) would split his time between* Grey's *and* Station 19. *The rest of the cast—Grey Damon, Barrett Doss, Alberto Frezza, Jay Hayden, Okieriete Onaodowan, Danielle Savre, and Miguel Sandoval—were largely unknown, although Sandoval had previously guest-starred as a patient on a season nine episode of* Grey's Anatomy. *The show launched as a backdoor pilot titled "You Really Got a Hold on Me" on March 1, 2018, during* Grey's *fourteenth season.*

Stacy McKee One of the things that I felt was really important with *Private Practice* and also with *Station 19* was that they be true ensembles. I thought it was nice to have a show that was called *Private Practice*, not *Addison Shepherd*. To me, that was a great thing for morale and for storytelling. It afforded you this ability to shift the focus at any point in the show. You could do entire episodes about other characters and it's all within that world. I wanted that flexibility. I really wanted it to be about this station and the people that come in and out of it.

The fans were only mildly impressed. Though then ABC Entertainment Group president Channing Dungey shared platitudes like, "No one can interweave the jeopardy firefighters face in the line of duty with the drama in their personal lives quite like Shonda," the network struggled to drum up interest in the drama in its first and second seasons, especially since Dick Wolf had already extended his Chicago *franchise by launching a hot fireman show of his own on NBC in 2012.* Station 19 *averaged fewer than 7.4 million viewers. Not eager to extinguish the drama just yet, ABC asked* Grey's Anatomy *showrunner Krista Vernoff to assume control of* Station 19 *starting in the third season, while McKee decided to move on to other opportunities.*

Stacy McKee It wasn't just two seasons. For me it was sixteen straight years of constant work. It was time. I really had done what I set out to do. I created a show that worked in the world that was a successful, thriving spin-off of *Grey's*. The entirety of my career had been under the Shondaland umbrella. It was just the right moment to branch out.

CHAPTER 6

"You Fought. You Loved. You Lost," Or, a Look Back at Some of the Most Polarizing Relationships on the Show

There's a reason why the original title sequence of *Grey's Anatomy* showed a man and woman lying together on a gurney and playing footsie behind a hospital curtain. Romance has always been the backbone of the show: even as doctors performed surgery, they babbled about their relationship status over an open cavity. It was both unreal and immensely entertaining, as if getting a guy to commit were just as important as removing a cancerous tumor.

Peter Horton *Grey's Anatomy* was mainly about who was in love with whom, who was having sex with who. When you think back on it, it was such an obvious idea. What a great way to do a hospital show!

Sara Ramirez (Dr. Callie Torres) To have these deep, disturbing medical cases and also have us laughing about our love interests is really powerful.

Jeannine Renshaw When you have such a huge cast, you're always juggling who's going to sleep with whom. I remember a lot of discussions about whether Callie was going to cheat on Arizona or if Arizona was going to cheat on Callie. For Alex it was always, "Who can he sleep with?" We always wanted him in a romance because he's so good at that. We would try to bring people in for him.

Stacy McKee It isn't specifically a show about hooking up, but of course when you have all of these different characters that are going to intermingle, you look for ways to see where different pairings can go. It was sort of open game. Usually at the end and beginning of each season we would have a brainstorming session, where we would throw all the spaghetti on the wall to see what might stick. Even if it's the most absurd thing you could ever consider on the planet, you throw it and you say, "Well, maybe? Let's think outside the box. What if those two people wound up in a relationship?" Sometimes you found the most unexpected pairings that worked out amazingly.

But for every perfect union on Grey's Anatomy, *there were an equal amount—if not more—of truly bad ones. Some of Rhimes's mating choices not only led to heated discussions in the writers' room, they drove fans to the brink of madness. The most egregious pairing in the history of the show was Meredith and 007, the nickname given to George after several of his early patients died. Hardly anyone was in favor of the one-nighter—viewers included—but that didn't stop Rhimes from throwing the pair under the sheets.*

Eric Buchman I remember the day that Shonda came in to say that Meredith was going to sleep with George. It was in season two and everyone thought that was way too soon. People are going to hate Meredith, because we knew they would never wind up together. It felt like it was too cruel a thing to do to George.

Tony Phelan Shonda and I had a screaming fight in the writers' room, where I told her that was a horrible idea. It was going to make Meredith totally unlikable, and she was going to lose the audience. Shonda likes nothing better than people pushing back at her. And she was like, "You're totally wrong. This is going to let the audience know that anything can happen and that characters are going to do things that are screwed up and wrongheaded. It'll be okay."

Jenna Bans I can picture Tony Phelan, like, gagging. He just hated them together and, you know, the show kind of played it that way. They played it for comedy. They played it that T. R. Knight's character was completely in love with Meredith, but from Meredith's point of view it was a mistake. We had those very distinct voices in the room. Some people thought it was completely natural and romantic because they were really, really close friends.

Ellen Pompeo It was shocking, even for me. I've been kissing Patrick since I met him, but I was like, "No, that's my T.! I can't make out with him!"

Sandra Oh When we saw that for the first time at a table read, we were like, "Noooo."

Mark Wilding I was in the camp that I didn't mind them sleeping together. I thought that was fine. I thought that's what made the show unique: people would watch these characters do these stupid things. They were very human in that regard. I remember during the second or third season of the show, seeing a billboard with all ten or eleven of the *Grey's Anatomy* doctors on the billboard. I remember thinking, Man, each of those characters has an individual personality. That's so rare on a television show, that they have flaws. They're just flawed people who, thank God, happen to be saving lives.

Stacy McKee I was on set for the episode where they wound up having sex and it was a challenge for all of us. We had to do it *twice*. I feel like it was a very human story, and in that way I really loved it. Who hasn't made strange choices in their sex life and who hasn't regretted a few of them?

Eric Buchman Shonda was insistent. It was like, "People make mistakes. Meredith is a real woman. It's a real mistake that she could really do: sleep with her best friend because you just lost the love of your life."

Shonda Rhimes When people say they hate what's happening, and then go on to describe in detail everything they hate, I know they're really paying attention and have strong feelings about the characters.

T. R. Knight George always [got] the short end of the stick. Thank God I didn't pine for [Meredith] for years.

Tony Phelan Shonda was absolutely right. And I learned a really valuable lesson, which is you need to get away from this idea of protecting this character. Protecting characters should be banned from any writers' room.—

Jenna Bans You need the show to have some longevity. They can't just live happily ever after from season four on. So I think we had a lot of heated discussions about who Derek and Meredith should be when they were not with each other.

Chandra Wilson We don't make apologies for anything. We're not the morality police.

James Pickens, Jr. The show takes you through these murky waters of these people's lives, and you come back because you want to see them heading north again.

George never found the love of his life before dying in season six, but he sure gave it the old college try—though with mostly disastrous results. In the first season, a casual hookup with Nurse Olivia led to a bad case of syphilis. Making matters worse, Olivia then slept with Alex and gave him the virus, too—which begat an uncomfortable amount of slut shaming around Seattle Grace.

Sarah Utterback Olivia had a major crush on George, who had a major crush on Meredith. There's the triangle! When I got rejected by him, I turned to Karev. And what I gathered from it was that Olivia regretted it. It was maybe out of rejection or wanting to feel better about herself. There's this scene between Karev and Olivia that's on my demo reel because I love it so much. It's a straight-on shot when they're in the break room, and he says, "It was good, right? It was simple. Easy." And I nod and I say, "Yeah." I don't know if he's referring to the sex or the rest of the flirtation, that it was a fun little fling. He was kind of hurt from Izzie, I was kind of hurt from George, so we found each other. That's okay for women to have, just as it's okay for men to have. But then what happened was we hooked up again and Izzie walks in and catches us. I have a scene right after where I'm apologizing to Izzie in the elevator. The [writers] decided it should be Olivia and not Karev [who apologizes]. It's reflective of how women internalize shame from sex. Saying "I have to apologize" and "I'm sorry for this." Why should she be sorry?

Joan Rater (Writer) Karev started as such an asshole, which he was.

Sarah Utterback It really is interesting that there was this character that I played who was shamed for her sexual experiences or desires. The world has changed a lot. Because of #TimesUp, I just don't think that this story line would happen [now].

George then moved on to Callie and demonstrated his affection by shooting Polaroids of her in surgery because he found her "sexy." The bloom quickly fell off the rose, in large part because of the disapproval of his fellow interns, Izzie included. But he still tied the knot with Callie in Las Vegas because it was his dad's dying wish, leading to an ill-fated marriage.

Shonda Rhimes He [had] been such a mess for so long, making weird choices.

Harry Werksman Because there was always that great unrequited love for Meredith, I think we felt that for a time, we'd sort of beaten him down so much emotionally. It was like, "Oh, this poor fucker, when is he gonna catch a break? He's just pining away for Meredith, and his little nurse girlfriend gave him syphilis. Callie, in many ways, was the antithesis of Meredith.

She's a big, bold, brassy, strong female character. Not that Meredith wasn't strong, but just physically they're very, very different. I think it was, "Let's get George a relationship that's gonna have some feet, some balls to it. Here's mild-mannered George and the man-eater, woman-eater Callie."

Tony Phelan There was something about Sara's character that was so annoying that we decided we were going to get rid of her very early. But then she had this secret sauce. As annoying as that character was, you felt something for her. That led us to say, "You know what? Let's really invest in her. Let's double down with the character." Sara's a very gifted actress and really had tremendous depth.

Jenna Bans I don't remember that. That's so funny. I always loved Callie.

Callie found the love of her life in Arizona, so it was hard for fans to see that relationship come to a heartbreaking end. Even worse, Callie began a surprise relationship with Dr. Penelope Blake, the doctor from Dillard Medical Center who'd failed to save Derek's life. In the episode "Old Time Rock and Roll," Callie surprised Meredith by bringing Penny to her dinner party. Mayhem ensued.

Samantha Sloyan Arizona and Callie were an incredibly beloved couple. Some people liked me, some people really didn't, and they're both right, you know? I thought that at the end of Penny's arc, she became a better doctor and a little bit more secure with herself. I think Callie was instrumental in that. She goes to New York and there's a little pep talk Callie gives her when she feels like the other girls are shutting her out. It was always, "I was a doctor from Dillard, and doctors from Dillard aren't good enough," and Callie was very good at making Penny believe that she was good enough and that she came to this hospital and was interning in order to get better. Because she knew that at the end of "How to Save a Life," she was never a good enough doctor and Meredith's husband was dead because she wasn't good enough to save him. I think Penny's whole journey was trying to become the best doctor she could be so she'd never be in that position again.

Rebound relationships were routinely doomed to failure in Seattle Grace—starting with Nurse Rose, played by Lauren Stamile. Rose was a perfectly lovely woman who caught Mc-Dreamy's eye in season two. But the poor gal never had a fighting chance.

Jenna Bans Fans *hated* Nurse Rose. And Nurse Rose is actually my very good friend! I went to college with her and she's the loveliest person and an amazing actress. But the fans just did not want Derek with anyone other than Meredith. So I remember we spent a long time in the room talking about, do we sort of bend to that pressure?

Lauren Stamile I got to kiss Patrick twice. The first episode we kissed, I was in my scrubs and had on that scrubs hat. I was like, "Oh, geez! Could you put me in something nicer? Could my hair at least be out?" Kissing scenes in general are not fun. They're really embarrassing and awkward. But he was such a professional. He always went out of his way to make sure I was comfortable. I think that it showed a strength of character for Rose to go. She accidentally hurt Derek in surgery. She gave him a scalpel and he got cut. I do not think that was on purpose. I think Rose was emotional and hurt and upset and angry.

Jessica Capshaw I actually auditioned for *Grey's Anatomy* four times. I first came to audition for the role of Nurse Rose who, die-hard *Grey's* fans know, was not well received. It was definitely destined to be a doomed role . . . and yet, I really wanted it.

Derek also went out on a date with Dr. Sydney Heron, a surgical resident from seasons two, three, and four who rubbed fans the wrong way because of her annoyingly perky disposition. Kali Rocha, the actress who played Sydney, said the match— however brief—was significant because it demonstrated that not every woman in the OR was hot for McDreamy.

Kali Rocha I dumped *him*! I told him that he wasn't ready. That was such a point of pride for me. I was like, "You know what? I can bring home the bacon. I can serve it up in a pan. *You're* not ready." That was so fun! Patrick was so delightful and was so tickled by me. He just went with it. He got what the dynamic was and how seriously Sydney took herself. I loved every minute of it.

Meredith, meanwhile, made a detour to Finn Dandridge (Chris O'Donnell), a veterinarian who'd lost his wife in a car accident. Finn was nice enough to escort Meredith to the Seattle Grace prom at the end of season two, and she repaid him by having sex with Derek in an exam room.

Stacy McKee It felt like the necessary next step for her character. I know there was such a rabid love for Meredith and Derek being together, but from a storyteller's perspective, happy couples get real boring real quickly. I know that fans don't see it that way 'cause they just want their people together, but part of the fun of a show is the yearning and the longing and just desperately wanting your people to get back together. If they were together all day every day, I know fans don't think they'll be bored, but they will be.

Chris O'Donnell It was always supposed to be an in-and-out thing. Then they kept asking me to stay for more episodes. I think at a certain point they wanted me to stay even longer, but having been in the business long enough, I knew it was never going to be *my* show. I mean, I was going to be so far down the totem pole. TV can be a great business, but you need to be able to participate in it. From a business standpoint, it just wasn't going to be *the* success for me. But what it did for me was incredible. It gave me an enormous boost. I was blown away by how many people were watching that show. It ultimately led to what I'm doing now [*NCIS: Los Angeles*]. So, I'm very grateful to Shonda and the team for the run. It opened up a lot of doors for me and kind of brought me back. I was in an uncomfortable place where I did not have a lot of job offers.

Even MerDer went through a sore patch with fans. Pulling them apart became just as interesting to Shonda Rhimes as keeping them together, so she tortured viewers with a will-they-won't-they courtship that imploded by the middle of season three—a plot point made worse by the 2007–2008

writers' strike. Pompeo, in particular, was not shy about voic-
ing her displeasure.

Ellen Pompeo I'm very much a believer in fate and chemis-try. When you meet a guy or a girl, chemistry takes over, and it doesn't really matter. So it's hard to judge characters. You can't, really, because that's when it gets really hard to play them. So you have to try to not be judgmental. But sometimes [Mere-dith] makes choices and you're like, "Why would she do this? Why would she continue to keep going back to him?" It's not always easy. The toughest for me to do is the relationship stuff with Patrick. Because it's the most repetitious, and if ever I judged anything, it has been the few things in the relationship. I would never let a man treat me that way, or I would never not value myself enough to be put in a situation that was painful.

Patrick Dempsey The writers were victims of their own suc-cess. They had confusion about how to resolve the dynamic, because the longing is what made it so interesting. But that doesn't sustain itself over four or five seasons.

Shonda Rhimes It was a tough year for all of us.

Ellen Pompeo I've got to be okay with whatever it is I have to do and find a way to make it real for the audience; to make the audience believe it. That's my only job. Whether they love my character or hate my character, if they're believing my per-formance, that's all I really care about. That's all I can control: my own performance. Otherwise I'd go crazy.

After Derek was killed off in season eleven, the writers in-
sisted on starting a new chapter for Meredith by pairing her

up with Dr. Nathan Riggs, played by Martin Henderson. But fans weren't ready for a McDreamy replacement, and neither was Pompeo. "The ink wasn't even dry on [Dempsey's] exit papers before they rushed in a new guy," Pompeo told The Hollywood Reporter *in 2018. "I was on vacation in Sicily, decompressing . . . and they're calling me going, 'What do you think of this guy?' And they're sending pictures. I was like, 'Are you people fucking nuts? Why do you feel that you have to replace this person?'"*

Martin Henderson When I got asked to come on and to sort of replace Patrick Dempsey as a love interest to Meredith, it was daunting. It wasn't lost on me that they were extremely big shoes to fill, and I think it would have been naive to think that I could have. I have so much respect for what he was able to do with that role and the position he held in the hearts of fans, you know? So it felt like a Herculean task, but then I sort of made peace with the fact that I wasn't there to be Derek Shepherd.

Ultimately, it was decided that Nathan's heart belonged to Owen's younger sister Megan (Abigail Spencer), so he was written off the show.

Martin Henderson My commitment to the show was always a shorter-term thing. I didn't sign a multiyear deal. I wasn't sure it was a show I would want to be on for too long. It was, in a way, a bit of an experiment, too. I think they were sort of trying to figure out what they were going to do with Riggs. I

think it was nice to have a character that brought a little different personality to the show, and to help Meredith navigate the
prospect of love on the heels of a death like that. So it felt like
an honor to play somebody who was pivotal in Meredith's life.
I know what she means to fans.

*It seems hard to believe, but Jackson and April, otherwise
known as Japril, were initially rejected by viewers.*

Jesse Williams (Dr. Jackson Avery) They hated April because she liked Patrick Dempsey's character. Fans hated me because I had been with Lexie. There's a lot of possessiveness with
fans. It's earned, and that's fine. People invest in these characters. But, you know, you're not supposed to like it right away.
It's supposed to be a weird fit. April and Jackson were opposites
in many ways. He was a suave, experienced guy in the romantic world. She was a virgin who was a bit of a spaz. We had a
year or two of our characters just being platonic. They were best
friends. I hesitate to say the chemistry was automatic, because
we really didn't get slammed together until a few years in.

Sarah Drew I think it took a minute for [fans] to jump on
the Japril train. I think there was also something really lovely
about the fact that they were just such solid friends. For us as
actors, we never had a hint or a whiff that our characters were
going to wind up together until the end of season eight. We
were just playing this relationship as close friends who tease
each other a lot and have each other's backs, but we never
played any of that, like, looking smolderingly at one another
and, "Oh, maybe something's going to happen!" There was

something kind of fresh about that. The audience didn't see it coming. They didn't know that was going to happen because it came out of absolutely nowhere.

Jesse Williams Fans were pretty well invested by "Japril the Movie." We got to go back in time and deal with some heavy stuff. We called it "Japril the Movie 1" and "The Sequel." Not to toot our own horn, but our scenes are the number one most-watched scenes on YouTube. They're obsessed with Japril. I don't often say the ship name, but I'm trying to be concise. I'm immediately regretting this decision.

Sarah Drew I didn't feel one way or the other about [the nickname]. I think I was just excited that people cared enough about the relationship that they gave us a name.

Once fans finally came around to Japril, anyone who threatened their love affair was pretty much dead on arrival. In other words, poor Matthew Taylor, the adorable paramedic who fell hard for April in season nine and treated her to a flash bomb proposal just a few weeks later. The two were literally about to say "I do" when Jackson, who attended the wedding with his new girlfriend, Stephanie (Jerrika Hinton), stopped the wedding.

Justin Bruening (Matthew Taylor) I always knew that my purpose during that time of the show was to get Jackson and April back together. I was sort of fighting a losing battle. I know how these things work. I did *All My Children* once. I was like, "So I'm basically here to get you two back together. That's great." I didn't realize she was going to leave me at the altar, though. That was just cruel!

Sarah Drew I know, it was awful. It was so epically romantic, so there's a lot about it that I love. But, like, we were horrible to our partners. That is the worst possible thing, and it feels so profoundly selfish to do something like that. So there were definitely mixed feelings, for sure. That's the other thing about April, is that she was such a rule follower her whole life, and this was a big moment where she's like, I'm going to follow my heart and maybe not do the right thing right now, because this is what I want. I don't know that it was the right choice, but she made it.

But Japril didn't last after the death of their infant son. Though April ultimately gave birth to their daughter, Harriet, she and Jackson divorced and he moved on to Maggie Pierce. April and Matthew ended up together, but in a hasty manner that had more to do with Sarah Drew's departure from the show in season fourteen.

Sarah Drew I think there are things that draw those two characters together that is wonderful, and I adore Justin Bruening. I do think there's a really lovely redemption story in all of that, in that she hurt him worse than anybody's ever hurt him in his life. Throughout the course of these years, she had a lot of pain and went through a lot of stuff, so they were able during this sort of broken and healing state to find each other again. He was able to forgive her. But I always, always wanted her to wind up with Jackson, especially after they had their baby. I wanted them to be this happy family unit, and I felt like the surprise marriage was rushed, to be honest. I just didn't believe it, because we hadn't seen anything on-screen between [April and] Matthew in that final season. I even wrote a very passionate letter to Krista after I read that final episode, saying, "Can she just walk off? Like, maybe kiss him and walk off into the distance doing something as an independent woman?" Like, why does she need a man? Why does she need that specific thing in this moment? Can't she just be her own human for a minute in her newfound return to faith and have new passion for working with the people experiencing homelessness? It just didn't feel like it was earned. But then Krista gave me all the reasons that I just mentioned, which was a full-circle redemption story, and I understood where she was coming from.

Justin Bruening I got stopped at the grocery store. I always do. They can't place where they know me and then I'll say, "It's probably *Grey's.*" Then they'll get wide-eyed and say, "Oh, yeah, we loved you when you were first on the show! To be honest, we want Jackson and April together." Thanks for that! I take it as a compliment.

Sarah Drew The other thing when you're making a TV show is that chemistry is not something you can just create. You either have it or you don't, and Jesse and I had really great chemistry together. That made people fall in love with us even more.

Justin Bruening I'm more than happy to take the back burner to Japril. I think that's fine. That's the love story. Two people who shouldn't be together, want to be together, and that's completely fine, even though I'm married to her now.

So I technically won. It took a long time, but I definitely won. Matthew and April have both been through so much sadness and pain. April lost her child and before that I lost my wife. All of a sudden it was like the playing field was even and leveled and they truly found comfort in each other. They found love again with each other through the midst of all that, and that's, I think, the whole point of her send-off as a character. Something came from it that ended up good. That feels to me like the ending April deserves.

CHAPTER 7

"There's an End to Every Storm," Or, How Katherine Heigl Went from Famous to Downright Infamous

Katherine Heigl became the drama's first actor to win an Emmy, beating out costars Sandra Oh and Chandra Wilson in the Outstanding Supporting Actress in a Drama Series category for the 2006–2007 television season. The then twenty-eight-year-old Heigl was completely deserving of the recognition, even though she admitted onstage at the 2007 Emmys that her mom didn't think she had a "shot in hell" of winning. As the interns of Seattle Grace would say: *Seriously?* Her scenes with Jeffrey Dean Morgan's Denny in season two alone were the reason why phrases like "water-cooler moments" were created in the first place.

Katherine Heigl Denny represented her dreams for the future, and she lost it all in seconds.

Jeffrey Dean Morgan (Denny Duquette) Denny and Izzie were lightning in a bottle.

Mark Tinker First of all, Jeffrey Dean Morgan was the nicest, sweetest, funniest guy, so he made it really easy. He and Katherine, from what I could tell, had a really good relationship. I had not been around for the setup of that relationship because it played over other episodes, and I'm not even sure I was able to look at those because they weren't even ready yet. I might've read some stuff, but it's very different when you read it compared to when you're actually on the set with the people who have lived in these characters. I do remember not being as invested in it as the people who had been there the whole time, including the crew. I do recall it was a very heavy moment when she got up there in that bed. It didn't feel at all macabre. It felt very natural and touching and sweet, and like you knew this was a moment in the show. This one was gonna resonate. When she was up on the bed there holding him, I remember getting choked up and I remember it choked the crew up. There was some sniffling going on.

Mimi Melgaard Izzie's dress was fantastic. I hadn't read the script yet. Shonda was writing it, and she said she wanted a very big dress for Izzie. That year in Los Angeles, all the dresses were very gauzy and long and soft. I'd fit Katie in dresses and Shonda would be like, "No, no. I want bigger." I was like, what? I searched and I couldn't find anything. We were in a real-time crunch because we *always* are on TV. So I called the wedding dress designer Amsale, and I was like, "Is there any way you could make me a wedding dress in pink, by next week?" And they were like, "We can do it." We picked the color of silk and FedExed back and forth. I picked the dress and redesigned the top and changed some things up. When you see the shot of Izzie in the elevator, and then Izzie lying across Denny, and then the shot of Alex holding her with her dress hanging down . . . those are the shots that Shonda saw in her head. That's why she wanted that big, beautiful princess dress that had its own voice within the story. Izzie was Cinderella for a minute. Then her heart was broken and bleeding all over Denny.

Stacy McKee I remember seeing Katherine with earphones on, listening to a song over and over to help keep her in that headspace.

Katherine Heigl You don't want it to be melodramatic and schmaltzy. [That was] one of the few opportunities I've had to be really challenged.

Nicole Rubio Katherine has an unbelievable talent in memorizing. Oh my God! She would be reading a book, and then we would say, "We're ready for you." She would stand in front of the camera, someone would say, "Rolling," she would put that doggone book in her lab coat, and then give you whatever you wanted. Then she'd be back to reading her book. She was crazy to watch. Some people who come to set are still trying to remember their lines. Katherine had no problem whatsoever.

Sarah Utterback There was such a beautiful chemistry and connection between Katie and Jeffrey. I remember the set being so quiet, like there was space for them to be full in their emotions. We knew this was something special. It was really moving and impressive to see these actors go there, take after take. They were endless with their emotional well. I was just blown away.

Stacy McKee Jeffrey never broke character. The two of them were just so in the moment and so committed.

Jeffrey Dean Morgan I can't remember a recent show where it caused such a reaction. Certainly Shonda Rhimes wasn't aware, so in hindsight she probably wouldn't have killed me. She brought me back, for God's sake! She called me in New York when I was on a movie. I said, "I'm dead! You know that, right?" But it was a no-brainer.

One New Jersey fan was so upset by Denny's death by stroke following a heart transplant that she tracked down the home number for writer Tony Phelan.

Tony Phelan [The caller exclaimed,] "How could you kill Denny?" It just shows you how invested people are. We're not listed anymore.

Mark Wilding I can remember my wife was like, "Don't tell me what happens." She couldn't watch it on Thursday night, so she said she'll watch it first thing the next morning. I said, "I don't know if you should." She goes, "I'll go to the grocery store and when I get home I'll watch the episode and see what happens." She's at the grocery store and all of a sudden a neighbor runs up to her and says, "Oh my God, I can't believe that Mark killed Denny!" It completely spoiled the surprise for my wife. I told her, but she didn't listen to me.

Mark Tinker The truth is that I haven't had people come up to me and geek out. There have been times when they've said,

"Oh, you did *Grey's*, huh?" Now that I know that scene was so iconic to people, I would say, "Yeah, that's right! I directed Denny's death," just to pull my suspenders out a little bit. I wasn't really aware until later that it had such an impact on people. Now I'm proud of having done it. I think I did it right.

Mimi Melgaard The dress had its own life! It went to Disney World in Florida for a long time. It goes on tour. That dress tours places! It's crazy. It's been all over.

Jeffrey Dean Morgan I will go to my grave knowing Denny changed my life.

It also had a profound effect on Izzie. So it was quite a jolt when Shonda Rhimes made the decision to follow up the iconic romance by pairing Izzie with George in season four— and while he was married to Callie.

T. R. Knight With George . . . and I loved playing him so much, but . . . he just tried so hard to be good, to do the right thing, and he constantly failed miserably. He really wanted to be a moral person, but then he ended up having affairs, hurting people, and doing the wrong thing.

Ellen Pompeo I loved Katie and T.R. so much that I didn't really like seeing them together. We see them together all the time anyway, because they're best friends. Katie and T.R. are adorable together. But, like, kissing? No! That's like my brother and my sister kissing. I don't want to see my brother and my sister kiss. I think that was a little ratings stunt.

Harry Werksman I think it came up in discussion and we were like, "Okay. Why not? Let's do that." Meredith couldn't sleep with everybody. People may think she did, and she did sleep with a lot of people, but no. I think we were just like, "Okay, that's a good idea and let's make it work." That was always how the room functioned, oftentimes it was Shonda who would come in and be like, "Hey, let's do this." Then it was our job to hunker down and figure out how it worked so it didn't look like, "Oh, gosh, let's put these two together because they haven't been together yet." It wasn't supposed to be like musical chairs.

Katherine Heigl I was really excited about it in the beginning because obviously I got to work more with my best friend and that's awesome. When I found out our little nickname was Gizzie, I knew it was over. I was like, "We're going to have to move on because that's not hot."

Stacy McKee You have to remember that so much of this stuff gets written and shot long before you get a reaction from fans, though we weren't anchoring our stories based on fan reactions. We were really anchoring our stories in the stuff that felt human or challenging or unexpected. Maybe people would like them or maybe people wouldn't. That's a real testament to Shonda, and one of her strengths in general. She didn't care if people didn't love it, she cared if we were telling good stories. And to me that's so important. Though in the moment that story was tough, I think those two characters were both so much stronger for it.

T. R. Knight To play this character who fought so hard to be this moral person and all of a sudden be doing one of the most immoral things . . . how do you wrap your mind around that? I never made any demands, like, "You do this, or else." I was always very respectful. In any sort of creative process, there are going to be disagreements.

Shonda Rhimes There could have been better communication.

That became a recurring theme for Heigl. The first break-down in talks actually began in 2007, when ABC Studios began renegotiating the salaries of the core group as a way to reward them for the show's early success. Heigl learned that the network was looking to give Ellen Pompeo, Patrick Dempsey, Sandra Oh, and Isaiah Washington bigger salary bumps so she made it public that she wasn't going to renegotiate her contract. Someone from her team even told People *how the studio "doesn't value her as much as her costars." ABC responded by saying that it had "approached Katherine with an offer to raise her compensation significantly above the terms of her current contract" and was "surprised to see this gesture reported negatively in the press." Heigl came back with the statement "I am embarrassed this has become a public matter." The matter was ultimately resolved when Washington was fired from the show; she got her money.*

Katherine Heigl In this town, women who don't just snap and say "Okay, yessir, yes, ma'am" start to get a reputation for being difficult. I've decided it's not worth it to me to be pushed around so much.

Former ABC Studios Executive Everyone has a sense of the value, what they're worth. Katie popped, but it was a different kind of pop. It was an ensemble piece, but the emphasis was on Ellen and Patrick and Isaiah and Sandra. When you took Isaiah out of the mix, it changed how the pay structure got done.

Person Familiar with the Situation The big issue with Shonda in those days—and by the way, she became a monster creator, she's unbelievably gifted as a writer and creator—was that she felt like the star of the show and resented that the actors were becoming stars of their own.

Harry Werksman As with all shows, success begins to breed petty differences, minor resentments that can always bubble below the surface. As time went on, you know, things change where we were suddenly like, "Whoa, look at that. We're the number one show in America. Oh, goodness, we won a Writers Guild Award. Wow. We just got nominated for an Emmy." You know, everyone was like, "Oh my God. How did that happen?" I think that affects everyone. I think it's just human nature.

Stephen McPherson *Grey's* wasn't as difficult as *Desperate Housewives* for sure. But I feel like the issues erupted all of a sudden.

Less than a year after winning her first Emmy, Heigl took what appeared to be a dig at Rhimes and the writers after a media outlet questioned why her name was missing from the nomination ballot. "I did not feel that I was given the material this season to warrant an Emmy nomination and in an effort to maintain the integrity of the academy organization, I withdrew my name from contention," Heigl said in a statement. "In addition, I did not want to potentially take away an opportunity from an actress who was given such materials." At the time, her comment was seen as a fairly overt attempt to leave the drama at the end of the 2008–2009 season so she could focus on a promising film career, given the success of Knocked Up *and* 27 Dresses.

Katherine Heigl The only thing I can really remember [about that season] is when I saved the deer. Shonda was always really great about giving me [Izzie's] backstory and telling me what she's thinking, [but] on the page sometimes you're like, "I'm sorry, what? What do you mean she's saving a deer? Wait, she's *shocking it back to life*?! Hold on now!"

Nicole Rubio She was young back then. She probably would have handled things differently [now]. But we all have our journey.

Tony Phelan There was a lot of attention on us and I think the actors all of a sudden, many of the younger actors lost their anonymity for the first time in their lives. And it was a real pressure cooker.

Katherine Heigl At the time I thought I was doing the right thing. And I wanted to be clear that I wasn't snubbing the Emmys. The night I won was the highlight of my career. I just was afraid that if I said, "No comment," it was going to come off like I couldn't be bothered [to enter the race]. But, really, I could have more gracefully said that without going into a private work matter. It was between me and the writers. I ambushed them, and it wasn't very nice or fair.

Brooke Smith She spoke to *Vanity Fair* and it sort of sounded like she was biting the hand that fed her, whenever she talked about Seth Rogen [and her time on *Knocked Up*].

There was truth to it. I mean, it was like a boys' club there. That's Judd Apatow for you. Then what followed, she had a season on the show where she didn't feel like there was enough meatiness to her role, so she didn't submit herself for the Emmys. It just came out the wrong way. I had a great time with her. I didn't have a single problem with her. Not one.

Katherine Heigl Everybody has bad days. I was a little defensive about my season because I thought I hadn't had a great one. And a lot of that had to do with me and my performances. I went into [Shonda's] office and I was just like, "Look, that was obnoxious. I apologize." And she was actually really supportive. She was like, "I get it. I totally get it. I know you didn't mean it like that."

Heigl continued her gaffe tour by appearing on The Late Show *with David Letterman and complaining about having just finished a long, seventeen-hour workday on the* Grey's *set. "I'm going to keep saying this because I hope it embarrasses them," she told Letterman. "A seventeen-hour day, which I think is cruel and mean." And when Letterman brought up how people were speculating when she would leave the show, Heigl replied sarcastically, "That's what I keep wondering."*

Katherine Heigl That was not the time or place to gripe about work. And when I watched it back, I was really embarrassed about how whiny I sounded. And I said it not once, but, like, *three* more times. I was really annoyed with myself after that one. That's when I realized, "Okay, look, Katie"—talking to myself like I sometimes do—"it's okay to be passionate. It's okay to have an opinion. But *filter*."

It was later revealed that—although poorly phrased—Heigl's complaints had to do with the crew's even longer hours rather than her own filming schedule.

Katherine Heigl I can suck up a seventeen-hour day. For them, that is not a fair thing to ask. They work their asses off and they don't get any of the accolades. They don't get any of the attention, and they don't get the paycheck. No one brought it up [when I got back to set] because I think they were all like, "Eh, Katie . . ." But there were some members of the crew who actually thanked me for saying something. Because they can't say anything.

Nevertheless, her reputation as an ungrateful diva had been burnished in the minds of fans, thanks to a barrage of negative headlines that occasionally bordered on cruelty. AOL News went with the headline "Grey's Beauty Has Ugly Mouth," while TMZ used "Paging Dr. UnGreyful—Get off Your Heigl Horse."

Mark Harris (Former executive editor/columnist) Really, if she'd said, "Actually, I *do* think my material should get me an Emmy nomination," would that sound better? I like the fact that she busted Isaiah Washington for homophobia when everyone behind the scenes at *Grey's Anatomy* was busy staring into space. I like the fact that she gently tweaked Judd Apatow for the slight gender imbalance in *Knocked Up.* I like the fact that her first thought after winning an Emmy wasn't, How can I get another one? And I like the fact that her mouth, which is not even slightly ugly, is connected to her brain.

Stephen McPherson I always thought that if you could

shoot these shows off in someplace where they're isolated, you would have less drama. You put these people in the spotlight, you put everyone under that pressure. It's one thing to be un-believable at your craft, but then we say, "Okay, now there's this whole other angle of dealing with the press and how you conduct yourself." They're used to living a private life and all of a sudden they've got people waiting by their mailbox, looking to get a picture of them in their underwear. It's hard, so I sym-pathize. As difficult as it was sometimes to be the executive in charge of all these shows and seeing all this drama, I do under-stand. It was not an easy situation to be in.

After Izzie was diagnosed with stage four metastatic mela-noma in season five, rumors swirled that Rhimes was looking to kill her off. Izzie survived, but Heigl failed to show up for work in March 2010. Eventually, it was decided that she would be released from her contract eighteen months early over family issues, not her burgeoning film career. There was truth to that: Heigl and her husband, Josh Kelley, had ad-opted their first child in 2009.

Katherine Heigl I started a family, and it changed every-thing for me. It changed my desire to work full time. I went on family leave and spent three months in Utah and just got to be a mom, and it changed my whole perspective . . . that was really the turning point for me. So before I was due back, I spoke again to Shonda about wanting to leave. Then I waited at home until I was given the formal okay that I was off the show. The rumors that I refused to return were totally untrue.

Tony Phelan People leave for a variety of reasons and I honestly do not fault anybody for wanting to leave the show because they'd been on the show for a really long time. And playing the same character for that long is its own challenge. And actors want to be challenged, actors want to do different things, and I don't fault anybody for that and the writers do the best they can.

Former ABC Studios Executive There could have been a happy medium there. She didn't want to leave the show. She just wanted a feature career.

Person Familiar with the Situation It had nothing to do with her film career. She wanted out because it was so hard working with Shonda.

Former ABC Studios Executive We could have found a way to keep her going for six to eight episodes [a year]. That would have created a different sort of imbalance with the other cast members. You would have had to weigh that.

Katherine Heigl [Shonda] wanted to try and figure out how I could do both [parenting and *Grey's*], and I kind of wanted to do both. But at the end of the day, there wasn't a great way to compromise the work schedule that didn't negatively affect the crew or the cast. It wasn't feeling fair to them or the show to ask them to bend around my needs.

Former ABC Studios Executive I think Steve McPherson and Shonda were just so fed up with it all, they just said, "Get her out."

Interest in Heigl was bigger than ever at that point, so it was a major coup that Entertainment Weekly *scored her only*

exit interview from Grey's Anatomy. *We tried to keep the*
cover hush-hush, but paparazzi were trailing Heigl when she
arrived at our photo shoot at Smashbox Studios in Los Ange-
les on March 20, 2010.

Henry Goldblatt We became the outlet that people came to
for these goodbye interviews. She dyed her hair brown the moment she stopped filming. I remember being annoyed that she
was not going to be recognizable to consumers on the newsstand.
"Who's that brown-haired woman who looks like Katherine
Heigl?" The cover that we ran was her with the prayer hands, and
she didn't want to do that originally. It was one of the last takes. It
went so well with the circumstances. It was hard not to use.

Richard Maltz (Former *EW* Photo Editor) She was hesitant
because she knew that would be the image that we would run.
She had just adopted a child, so maybe that's why the paparazzi
were stalking her. They were like climbing up on the gate wall
to get shots of her.

Michael Ausiello [Doing that cover] was one of the highlights of my time at *EW.* I flew out to L.A. and spent an afternoon
with Katherine at her house. She treated me like royalty, with
cheese plates and champagne and cookies, all of which I was
too nervous to consume. The interview went really well. She was
funny, disarming, humble, and very forthcoming. It was a great
experience. And the cover photo—which was a shot of Katherine
clasping her hands in prayer while looking skyward—tied in perfectly with the apologetic tone she struck during the interview.
She was not a fan. She went on David Letterman a week later and
said she hated that we went with that image.

For Heigl's final episode, Izzie returned to Seattle Grace to get one last scan to prove she's cancer-free. She hoped she and Alex could reunite, but he tells her he "deserves someone who will stay."

Jenna Bans I remember discussing whether we would kill her off. And in the end she left after being cured of cancer because I think, to my memory, Shonda felt like that was more of an unexpected way to go. The second the audience sees a character has cancer, they're like, "Oh, she's leaving, this is how they're getting rid of her." So she wanted to sort of twist it at the last moment.

Mark Wilding I don't know why we didn't kill Izzie, I really don't. I don't know if there was a hope in all our minds that she might come back to the show. Katie subsequently talked about wanting to maybe come back to the show to wrap things up a couple years later, but that never happened. We didn't kill everybody. Burke lived. He went on to a hospital in Switzerland.

Katherine Heigl I felt it was the right thing to do; we just didn't quite know how to do it appropriately, gracefully, and respectfully to the audience. I think we all felt that it *wasn't* respectful to the audience to bring [Izzie] back again and then have her [leave] again. We did it twice. It starts to feel a little manipulative.

Nicole Rubio I didn't really know she was leaving until she was actually leaving.

Moe Irvin I don't think I was aware it was her last show. I didn't get info the way the regulars did. At that point I don't think I was getting full scripts, either, to avoid script leaks. So technically that episode was the last time I saw her. I'm sure I said goodbye normally, not knowing that would be her last episode.

Robert Baker I had no idea [she was leaving] and I don't know how much anybody else really did. She was always supposed to leave for a certain amount of time to do a movie. I can't remember what movie, but she was doing something. So I think that was always kind of baked into the season, that she would get fired and then would come back for some reason. Then she just kind of never came back. And then, my character's story line was kind of tied to her, so when she was done, so was I, I think. Katie and I got along great. When I got the gig there were a lot of warnings from a lot of people about a lot of people on the show, but I didn't have a problem with anybody, honestly. She and I got on quite well. Her husband grew up not far from where I did, so he and I got on. So yeah, she and I got on just fine.

Person Familiar with the Situation I'm not saying she was the most user-friendly person, but I think Katie got a raw deal. There were really two sides to that story. Katie was just beaten up for having an opinion, beaten up for being successful, beaten up for not kissing the ring. She became much bigger than Patrick Dempsey, but she didn't have a penis.

Katherine Heigl I just had to make a choice. I hope I made the right one . . . it sucks. You wish you could have it all exactly the way you want it. But that's not life [and] I had to try to find the courage to move on. . . . The ungrateful thing bothers me the most. And that is my fault. I allowed myself to be perceived that way because I was being whiny and I was griping and because

I made these snarky comments. So much about living life, to me, is about humility and gratitude. And I've tried very hard to have those qualities and be that person and I'm just so disappointed in myself that I allowed it to slip. Of course. Of course I'm grateful. How can I not be grateful?

Where did I go wrong?
I lost a friend
Somewhere along in the bitterness
And I would have stayed up with you all night
Had I known how to save a life.

—"How to Save a Life," the Fray

No song is more appropriate for the drama on *Grey's Anatomy* than "How to Save a Life," a melancholy ballad from the Fray's debut studio album of the same name that was released in September 2005. After music supervisor Alexandra Patsavas saw the band perform in Los Angeles, she licensed the song to score a montage of surgery scenes in episode twenty-two of season two. The song, which was also performed by the entire cast in "Song Beneath the Song" and served as the title of Derek Shepherd's final episode, went triple platinum and remains the Fray's highest-charted tune to date.

Isaac Slade (Lead Vocals, Piano) I remember I was on a trip to England and was really struggling with a buddy of mine who was making bad choice after bad choice. I was standing in a swimming pool and saw a placard that said: "How to rescue a victim." It had eight colored drawings that said things like "First you do this." I remember staring at that, thinking, Man, wouldn't it be awesome if there was one of those for real life? *If your wife doesn't love you, do this! If your kid won't call you back after your alcoholic rage, follow these easy steps to restore the relationship!* I remember thinking, Wouldn't it be awesome if it was that easy? I wrote it on a little scrap of paper: *how to save a life.* It was like, how to save the lives you love.

Joe King (Guitar, Backup Vocals) We couldn't write anything that was super happy. It was difficult for us. Some of us are great at that, having a candy kind of song. I wish we could have done that. But it always felt cheesy and contrived when we did it. We would write what we were angry about, what we were questioning. It was about being real.

Isaac Slade My most vivid memory was recording it. That's what rocked me. The guys all left and it was just me and Joe in the studio with our producer. The studio was this little rock haven in Bloomington, Indiana. One of John Mellencamp's guys set up a studio there. It was cold and dark and woodsy. "How to Save a Life" was a hard song to write. The song is supposed to be ironic. You can't just write a formula. I was recording the vocals and kept breaking down. I remember Joe came in and gave me this huge hug. We just chatted for a few minutes and then I sang the vocal that's on the record. We recorded the drums with towels and the piano was super quiet. I remember thinking it was going to be, like, track twelve on the album. It hadn't even crossed my mind that it would be some big song. I wanted to

tuck it in at the end when no one was looking. It was just the
one that made me cry. It was wrecking me, so maybe it was going to connect with other people, too. That's the memory that
stands out the most to me. It was from something Joe and I . . .

Joe King . . . we had gone to a troubled teens camp, a rehab center. It took teens from all over the country.

Isaac Slade Everybody was court mandated to be there. It
was after a plea bargain, kind of an "if you don't go to jail,
you go to this kind of place." It was a bunch of fourteen-to
eighteen-year-old kids.

Joe King They just asked us, "Would you guys want to come
up to volunteer and mentor some of the kids?" We had just
started the band. I don't remember exactly what we did, maybe
some group meetings. We just kind of hung, kind of casual.
There was a kid who really opened up. We started talking to him
about his story and how he went to different rehab facilities. He
was maybe seventeen. He had been a heavy addict for five years.

Isaac Slade He had finally kicked heroin. I was like,
"What?"

Joe King He was the nicest kid, too. He was very open and
honest, like, "Yeah, man, I don't know how to kick this thing.
Every time I finish a treatment, I get out and I just fall back
into it." We were clearly moved by his story. We just didn't
know what to say. Here's a seventeen-year-old who's had a very
hard life, and I was at a loss for words. I didn't want to give
him some easy answer like, "You've just got to do this!" That's
my tendency when someone is opening up. You want to fix it.
That was the impetus of the song. It was more about: How do
you find hope, how do you find redemption, how do you find

yourself coming from a place of extreme addiction? The song was really birthed from not knowing what to do or what to say to someone who was in extreme need. The song was meant to be a question. To this day, I don't know if I have more answers than questions.

Isaac Slade We invited that kid to shows. I hung at his house and met his mom. He had a big, five- or six-year period where he was doing awesome. He was really working hard, had a great girlfriend. I thought, Who knew? Somewhere around our third record, he started nosediving again. He landed in jail after robbing some store. Then his phone number stopped working. We certainly didn't intend for that outcome. But I think that outcome is significant because it doesn't always end like a happy movie. That's the point: there is no guarantee that if you love somebody, it's going to work out. If you write the song right, it's universal, and everybody can find their own thoughts in it. I remember somebody came up to us and said it was their wedding song. And then shortly after that, somebody came up and said their son took his own life and this is what they played at his funeral. I just remember thinking, That's what we were doing it for, to make something that people can find themselves in, to get something from it, to keep going.

Joe King "Over My Head (Cable Car)" was our first single from the *How to Save a Life* album.

Isaac Slade We went platinum from "Over My Head." We opened for Weezer.

Joe King The single had been out for a good year, and then that summer, "How to Save a Life" was slotted as the second single. Looking back, the timing was essential. If "How to Save a Life" was our first single and had the tie to *Grey's*, I don't know if we would have had much of a run after that. It would have been so synonymous with the show. People wouldn't have seen us as a legitimate band.

Isaac Slade It wasn't quite cool yet. Any rock star that talks about licensing is like, "No, man, you're supposed to change the world." I remember in the back of my head thinking, Are my friends going to make fun of me?

Joe King It was unknown territory. We weren't sure if this was going to kill our career. As an artist you want to protect your songs, these babies that you've written, and not crush your career by making the wrong decision. It was crippling to think about.

Isaac Slade I was driving from Denver to Fort Collins with my brother. We were in the car for an hour and I asked, "Have you ever seen *Grey's Anatomy*?" My brother was like a rugby player and a repo man at the time, a total rough-and-tumble cat. And he was like, "Oh, yeah, I've seen *Grey's*. That show hits me every time." He described this scene to me and then two grown-ass men were driving down the road with tears running down our faces. I remember wiping my tears away, thinking, Man, we should probably do this. If my brother watches it, it's probably something good.

Joe King I don't remember watching the episode. I don't remember the exact scene it was used.

Isaac Slade I guarantee someone died.

Joe King I remember feeling, like, Whoa, this is big. It felt like everything was going to change.

Isaac Slade I remember vividly sitting in your living room, thinking, Oh, we're in a partnership with these people. They want their show to be good, too. It was art! It was beautiful and powerful and moving, right up to the edge of cheesy without going over that edge. The formula worked. Oh! Okay. Licensing is cool.

Joe King We were touring theaters.

Isaac Slade We went triple platinum. We were like, "We've got to get bigger rooms!" We went to the Grammys. "How to Save a Life" was nominated. [The song lost to "Dani California" from the Red Hot Chili Peppers in the Best Rock Performance by a Duo or Group with Vocal category.]

Joe King There was probably a little part of me that pushed against any kind of corporation sellout or TV connection, but when I stepped back and got perspective, I thought, I'm playing music with my buddies! This is a dream! Hell, we get to go tour the world! How can I complain? These will be stories I can tell my grandchildren. Our life was just a whirlwind. We were touring on our first record for two and a half years. We played for presidents. We played "How to Save a Life" for Pope Francis at the Festival of Families in Philly. It was his first trip to the U.S. They asked us, along with Aretha Franklin, Andrea Bocelli, and Jim Caviezel. You know, Jesus.

Isaac Slade He's one of the sweeter Jesuses I've met.

Joe King It's not like we had this goal and intention to change the game in music licensing. For some reason the timing all worked out. The industry at that point was looking for new ways to break artists, and TV became a way to break a single.

Isaac Slade I do remember a lot of people I met, they would

say they heard about us from the show. That was common, especially among women in their twenties and thirties. I felt like
I should have minded, but I didn't. I'm an impact guy. I'm not
drawn to fame or fortune for the dollars. I'm definitely drawn
to that stuff for the impact, the reach of our art. So to me, *Grey's*
felt like one hundred percent a slam dunk. It got this really
emotional song in front of a huge audience on a consistent
basis that amplified our little idea on a nuclear bomb level. I
remember feeling kind of guilty because it was so big, in the
chutes and ladders sense, since we had only been a band for
four years at that point. *We didn't pay our dues enough. We're
supposed to be slogging away in the trenches for twenty years!* I felt a
little guilt about that. But when someone tells you they heard it
on *Grey's Anatomy,* I was like, "Sweet!"

CHAPTER 8

"He's Very Dreamy, but He's Not the Sun," Or, How *Grey's Anatomy* Loved — Then Learned to Live Without — Patrick Dempsey

Ellen Pompeo may have played the titular role, but for many fans over many years, Patrick Dempsey was the real draw to *Grey's Anatomy.* Some of it had to do with his celebrity: Dempsey was the most famous member of the original cast at the time of the pilot and brought with him quite a cult following from his 1987 movie *Can't Buy Me Love.* But a lot of it was due to the way Rhimes wrote her McDreamy and how Dempsey depicted him.

James D. Parriott I would say, "The guy would never say that," and Shonda would say, "He's McDreamy. He's the perfect man. He *would* say that." I'd say, "Okay. It's your show."

Eric Buchman Shonda had a very clear idea of how important it was to keep Derek as this almost idealized love interest, not just for Meredith but for the audience. Naturally, the writers—especially writers who had been working on one-hour dramas for a while—were like, "Well, maybe have Mc-Dreamy make a big mistake in surgery and kill somebody. Or he develops an addiction of some kind. What is his deep, dark secret?" Shonda was very insistent: that's not the character we do that with. Even when you find out he's married, that was done in a very sympathetic way that kept him being a hero. He was wronged by his spouse and in spite of it all he was still gonna give his marriage a second chance.

Stacy McKee Shonda was protective of McDreamy, but it was really with an eye toward being protective of Meredith. I don't think the two were separate from one another. I don't think she wanted to put something out there that maybe on the surface might seem a little frivolous. At its core, there was something really substantial that she wanted to say. She wanted to be very specific about the type of relationship values that she put out there.

Tony Phelan I was in editing with Shonda once, and it was the scene where Meredith and Derek had broken up. He comes over and she's like, "I can't remember the last time we kissed." And he says, "I remember. You were wearing this and you smelled of this . . ."

Joan Rater "Your shampoo smelled like flowers, you had that sweater on . . ." He described their last kiss.

Tony Phelan Typically in editing you start on Derek, then you cut to Meredith for a reaction, and then you'll go back to him. I noticed that we weren't ever cutting back to Meredith. I asked why. Shonda said, "Because the woman in Iowa who's watching this show wants to believe that Patrick is talking to her, and if you cut back to Meredith, it pushes them out of it." In those special moments, we would just lock into Derek and let him do his thing.

Joan Rater And he was a master at it.

Patrick Dempsey He's the ideal man, and that's what Shonda constructed. There's a projection [of him] onto me when you come in contact with fans, certainly with the younger and older fans. There is a certain amount of expectation. There is a responsibility to it. It made me grow, too. There were good qualities [of his] that you work on to obtain.

Off camera, Dempsey was equally as charismatic to his fellow actors, crew members, and anyone who would come to visit the set.

Lauren Stamile I was going in to meet him, and I remember I had this little cardigan sweater on and I took it off before I got into the room. Dempsey is one of those people—it's almost like there's a light shining around his body, and you feel like you're the only person in the room. I got so hot and I remember saying, "Gosh, I would take off my sweater if I had one on because I'm so hot, but I took it off." I was just babbling. He said, "You look nice," and I said, "You look nicer." I felt so awkward and he was so gracious and lovely. I was having a nervous breakdown. It's like this "it" factor. I was like, God, whatever he has, I wish I had. I think it was very obvious how nervous I was, and he went out of his way to make sure he introduced me to everybody and made sure I felt comfortable, which he certainly didn't have to do. But he did.

Joan Rater He knew I had a giant crush on him, and he loved it. And when we'd go to table reads—I was an actress at one point in my life—they would always give me Meredith if Ellen wasn't there. And I'd be getting my chicken tenders at craft services before the table read and he'd come up behind me and say, "Are you reading Meredith?" in my ear, like, so sexy. I'd be like, Oh my God. I mean, I could barely . . . I could not look at him.

Tina Majorino I worked with Patrick a ton. I love him so much. We had a really great time working together. I think he's such a great actor and he really made me laugh a lot. I feel like we had a good dynamic in scenes together, and it was always fun to play opposite him. Yes, he's that charismatic in real life. Yes, his hair is that awesome. Yes, he is dreamy up close.

Chandra Wilson Patrick Dempsey will forever be known as *Grey's Anatomy*'s McDreamy. Derek Shepherd is a permanent part of television history.

Norman Leavitt He is a big, personable guy.

Jeannine Renshaw We all love Patrick. Patrick is a sweetheart. If I saw him on the street, I'd give him a hug. I love the guy.

Mark Wilding I've always had a soft spot for Patrick. He really does try to do the right thing.

Brooke Smith, who played Dr. Erica Hahn, remembers how Dempsey defended her when the decision was made to fire her from the show in 2008.

Brooke Smith I remember calling him and saying, "Oh my God, they said they can't write for me anymore, so I guess I'm

The cast of *Grey's Anatomy* from 2006.

(Photo by Bob D'Amico, courtesy of Walt Disney Television via Getty Images)

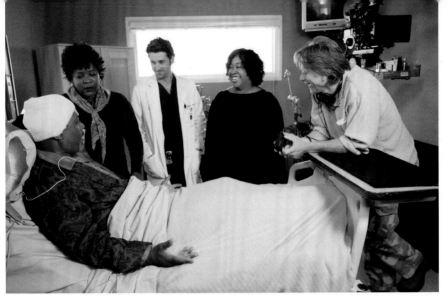

Executive producers Shonda Rhimes and Peter Horton with James Pickens, Jr., Loretta Devine, and Patrick Dempsey.
(Photo by Craig Sjodin, courtesy of ABC/Walt Disney Television via Getty Images)

Monica Keena (Bonnie) and Bruce A. Young (Tom) were memorably impaled on a pole during "Into You Like a Train," a season 2 episode from 2005 that earned Krista Vernoff an Emmy nomination for Outstanding Writing for a Drama Series.
(Courtesy of ABC)

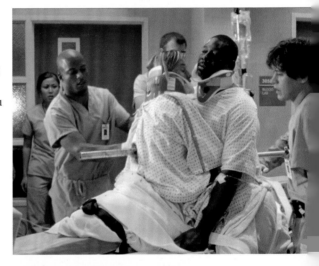

Izzie weeps in the arms of her beloved Denny Duquette in the season 2 finale, "Losing My Religion."
(Courtesy of ABC)

Katherine Heigl (Izzie Stevens) receives the show's first Emmy for acting in 2007.
(Photo by Kevin Winter, courtesy of Getty Images)

The inimitable Derek Shepherd, aka McDreamy, played by Patrick Dempsey.
(Photo by Gail Adler, courtesy of ABC/Walt Disney Television via Getty Images)

Meredith (Ellen Pompeo) removed a bomb from a man's torso before handing it over to defuser Dylan Young (Kyle Chandler) in the memorable "As We Know It" episode from season 2.

(Photo by Peter "Hopper" Stone, courtesy of Walt Disney Television via Getty Images)

Kate Walsh graces *EW*'s Fall Preview cover on September 14, 2007.

The cast of *Private Practice,* the first spinoff of *Grey's Anatomy* that launched in 2007. (Photo by Eric Ogden, courtesy of ABC/Walt Disney Television via Getty Images).

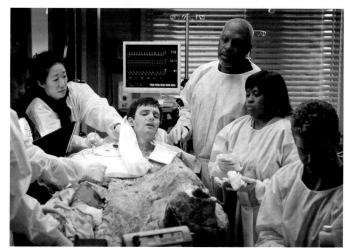

In the season 4 two-parter dubbed "Freedom I and II," James Immekus played a hapless teen named Andrew who jumped in a vat of cement to impress a girl. (Photo by Michael Desmond, courtesy of Walt Disney Television via Getty Images)

George O'Malley (T. R. Knight) was fatally injured beyond recognition at the end of season 5 but fans were treated to a beautiful last image of him as he quietly gazes at his soul sister Izzie. (Courtesy of ABC)

T. R. Knight on the cover of
EW, July 31, 2009.

Katherine Heigl gave *EW* an
exclusive exit interview for the
April 2, 2010 issue.

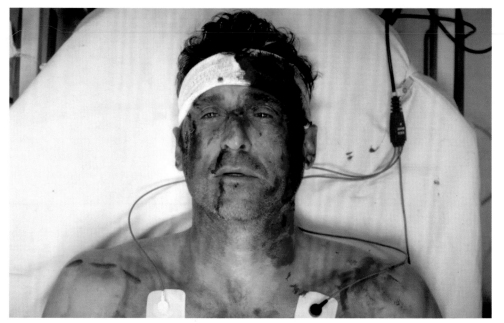

Since a horrific accident left him without the ability to speak, Derek was forced to watch inept doctors make poor decisions that ultimately led to his death in "How to Save a Life" in 2015. (Courtesy of ABC)

Shonda Rhimes becomes the first female showrunner to appear on an *EW* cover (alongside her stars Ellen Pompeo, Viola Davis, and Kerry Washington), for the September 11, 2015 issue.

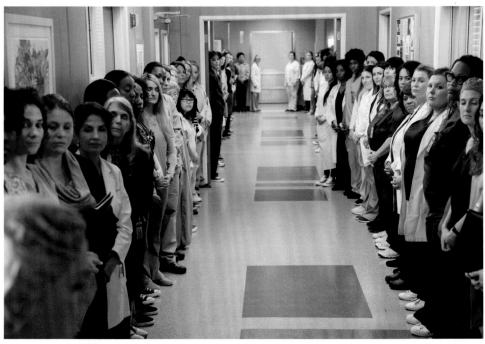

In season 15, showrunner Krista Vernoff, director Debbie Allen, and writer Elisabeth R. Finch created a heart-wrenching standalone episode about a victim of sexual assault. "Silent All These Years" culminated with an outpouring of love and support from the women of Grey Sloan.

(Photo by Mitch Haaseth, courtesy of Walt Disney Television via Getty Images)

Ellen Pompeo, cover girl (again!), for *EW*'s Sept. 28, 2018 issue.

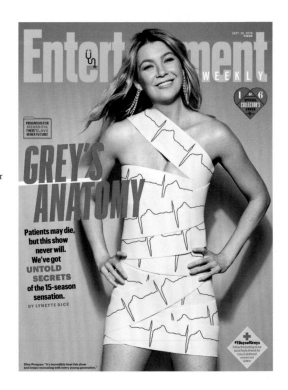

leaving." And he was like, "What are you talking about? You're the *only* one they're writing for." Which at that time, it kind of did feel that way. But I guess someone didn't like that. They gave me a statement [to release, about her departure] and I never said it. Patrick said that he actually took it out of his jacket on *The Ellen DeGeneres Show* and read the statement. He won't let me forget it. He was like, "I defended you, see?" And it was true.

By season eleven, however, fans saw a disturbing break in MerDer's once unbreakable bond. Six episodes had gone by without a peep from Derek, who was supposedly in Washington, D.C., where he had apparently made out with a research fellow. Fans began threatening to bolt if their hero didn't return soon to Seattle. "I have never missed one episode," wrote a fan on Dempsey's Facebook page. "But I swear if [Rhimes] kills you off I'm done." But there was a critical reason for Derek's strange absence: behind the scenes, there was talk of Dempsey's diva-like fits and tension between him and Pompeo. To help manage the explosive situation, executive producer James D. Parriott was brought back in to serve as a veritable Dempsey whisperer.

Patrick Dempsey [That] was the first year that I haven't been in every episode. I [was] in every episode since the pilot—close to 250 episodes. That [was a] huge run.

James D. Parriott Shonda needed an OG to come in as sort of a showrunner for fourteen episodes. There were HR issues. It wasn't sexual in any way. He sort of was terrorizing the set. Some cast members had all sorts of PTSD with him. He had this hold on the set where he knew he could stop production and scare people. The network and studio came down and we had sessions with them. I think he was just done with the show. He didn't like the inconvenience of coming in every day and working. He and Shonda were at each other's throats.

Jeannine Renshaw There were times where Ellen was frustrated with Patrick and she would get angry that he wasn't working as much. She was very big on having things be fair. She just didn't like that Patrick would complain that "I'm here too late" or "I've been here too long" when she had twice as many scenes in the episode as he did. When I brought it up to Patrick, I would say, "Look around you. These people have been here since six thirty A.M." He would go, "Oh, yeah." He would get it. It's just that actors tend to see things from their own perspective. He's like a kid. He's so high energy and would go, "What's happening next?" He literally goes out of his skin, sitting and waiting. He wants to be out driving his race car or doing something fun. He's the kid in class who wants to go to recess.

Patrick Dempsey It's ten months, fifteen hours a day. You never know your schedule, so your kid asks you, "What are you doing on Monday?" And you go, "I don't know," because I don't know my schedule. Doing that for eleven years is challenging. But you have to be grateful, because you're well compensated, so you can't really complain because you don't really have a right. You don't have control over your schedule. So, you have to just be flexible.

Longtime Crew Member Poor Patrick. I'm not defending his schtick. I like him, but he was the Lone Ranger. All of these actresses were getting all this power. All the rogue actresses would go running to Shonda and say, "Hey, Patrick's doing this. Patrick's late for work. He's a nightmare." He was just shut out in the cold. His behavior wasn't the greatest, but he had nowhere to go. He was so miserable. He had no one to talk to. When Sandra left, I remember him telling me, "I should've left then, but I stayed on because they showed me all this money. They just were dumping money on me."

Patrick Dempsey It [was] hard to say no to that kind of money. How do you say no to that? It's remarkable to be a working actor, and then on top of that to be on a show that's visible. And then on top of that to be on a phenomenal show that's known around the world, and play a character who is beloved around the world. It's very heady. It [was] a lot to process, and not wanting to let that go, because you never know whether you will work again and have success again.

Jeannine Renshaw A lot of the complaining . . . I think Shonda finally witnessed it herself, and that was the final straw. Shonda had to say to the network, "If he doesn't go, I go." Nobody wanted him to leave, because he *was* the show. Him and Ellen. Patrick is a sweetheart. It messes you up, this business.

James D. Parriott I vaguely recall something like that, but I can't be sure. It would have happened right toward the end, because I know they were negotiating and negotiating, trying to figure out what to do. We had three different scenarios that we actually had to break because we didn't know until I think about three days before he came back to set which one we were going to go with. We didn't know if he was going to be able to negotiate his way out of it. We had a whole story line where we were going to keep him in Washington, D.C., so we could separate him from the rest of the show. He would not have to work with Ellen again. Then we had the one where he comes back, doesn't die, and we figure out what Derek's relationship with Meredith would be. Then there was the one we did. It was kind of crazy. We didn't know if he was going to be able to negotiate his way out of it. It was ultimately decided that just bringing him back was going to be too hard on the other actors. The studio just said it was going to be more trouble than it was worth and decided to move on.

Stacy McKee I don't think there was any way to exit him without him dying. He and Meredith were such an incredibly bonded couple at that point. It would be completely out of character if he left his kids. There was no exit that would honor that character other than if he were to die.

Patrick Dempsey I don't remember the date [I got the news]. It was not in the fall. Maybe February or March. It was just a natural progression. And the way everything was unfolding in a very organic way, it was like, "Okay! This is obviously the right time." Things happened very quickly. We were like, "Oh, this is where it's going to go."

So that was that: McDreamy would die in episode twenty-one of season eleven, even though Dempsey was in year one of his recently signed two-year contract extension. Rhimes wrote a script that was befitting of her lead's heroic persona: she began "How to Save a Life" by having Derek witness a car crash and helping the injured. Once it appeared everyone was out of harm's way, Derek continues on his road trip but is suddenly broadsided by a truck.

Rob Hardy (Director) The paramedics leave. He's there by himself. He's having a moment. The nice music is playing, and all of a sudden, *bang.* It comes out of nowhere, which, you know, is how accidents happen. So as opposed to watching it as a viewer, we saw the accident happen through Derek's perspective.

Derek ends up at Dillard Medical Center, a hospital far from Grey Sloan and the talented doctors who work there. His eyes are open, but his brain is severely damaged. No one hears his plea for a CT scan; he can't speak. To help keep the episode a secret, the scenes were shot in an abandoned hospital in Hawthorne, California, about twenty-two miles from the show's home studio in Los Feliz.

Mimi Melgaard It was really hard on all of us because it was so secretive and we had so many different locations. We shot at this closed-down hospital that was absolutely creepy haunted. All the scenes there were so sad anyway, and in this yucky-feeling haunted hospital? It was really weird. His whole last episode was really tough.

Patrick Dempsey It was like any other day. It was just another workday. There was still too much going on. You're in the midst of it—you're not really processing it.

Rob Hardy Here's a guy who's immobile. Now you're inside of his head. We were trying to make that feel scary from the perspective of a person who's used to being in control, from a person who usually has the power of life and death in his own hands. But now he doesn't have the ability to speak on his own behalf.

Samantha Sloyan When I went to audition, I didn't recognize any of these doctors' names. I assumed they were just dummy sides so people wouldn't ruin the story line or anything like that. All we knew is that we were dealing with a man who's been in a car accident. I had no idea that it was going to be Derek. I just figured I was going to be a guest doctor and that whoever this person was who was injured, was going to be just a character on the show. Once it became clear what we were working on, I was like, Oh, my gosh. *I can't believe this is the episode I'm on.*

Mike McColl (Dr. Paul Castello) I signed an NDA before they would release the script to me. I was reading it in my house, and I was like, "Oh, my God." I didn't tell anyone, including my agents. I just said, "This is a really great booking. It's a great role on *Grey's.*" And they didn't know anything until it aired.

Savannah Paige Rae (Winnie) The first scene I shot was actually the sentimental scene when I'm saying, "It's a beautiful day to save lives, right?" I'm in the hospital room with Derek and talking to him. Even though I never watched the show, I recognized the value of the episode I was in and just really took it to heart. It was so special that I got to be a part of it.

Rob Hardy [Patrick] had a lot of emotions during the whole shoot, which evolved. I think when we first started, he was very calm and cool . . . the same Patrick that I remembered when

I worked on the show a year or so before. With each passing day, he was a lot more emotional. A lot more was on his mind, and that would show itself in different ways. The finality of the episode and for his character was setting in. You've become a global icon on this show and then in five, four, three, two, a day . . . it's over.

James D. Parriott Patrick was very cooperative and good.

Mike McColl When I met Patrick, he's lying on a stretcher and we're rushing him into the ER. I just introduced myself, shook his hand, and was like, "Man, I cannot tell you what an honor it is to be the guy to take you down." He loved it. He could not have been nicer to me and was funny through the whole shoot. He was on the table in front of me there when I cut his chest open and all that stuff. He gave me a hug at the end. It was a real privilege to be a part of TV history in that way.

Samantha Sloyan I remember him being incredibly kind. They had his neck in a brace, and he's strapped down to the board, so there wasn't a ton of chatting. I remember him being really kind, but it was clearly intense for him.

Stacy McKee It was such a beautiful piece of storytelling. I knew this event was going to be a really sad, horrible event for Meredith, but I also knew it was going to be the beginning of such an incredible chapter for Meredith.

Dempsey completed his final hours of shooting on a rainy night. There was no goodbye party, no goodbye cake. Maybe that's because some cast members were left out of the loop. James Pickens, Jr., told ABC News that the cast "didn't know

a whole lot. It was kind of on the fly. So whatever informa-
tion we got, we pretty much got it kind of right before it
happened."

Caterina Scorsone (Dr. Amelia Shepherd) I didn't get to
say goodbye to Patrick when he left. I do think that helped,
because I've been using the character of Derek in my internal
landscape since *Private Practice.* Derek was the stability in Amelia's life. He became a father figure after they watched robbers
shoot their father. When he was suddenly gone from the show,
we didn't have that closure, so I got to play it out. She's about
to use drugs again before Owen confronts her in a way that she
finally talks about her feelings about losing Derek. She doesn't
end up using.

James D. Parriott The day he left, that was my last day.
There was a certain sadness to it, but I think he was relieved. I
mean, I think it took a toll on him, too.

Rob Hardy I didn't see other actors showing up and saying,
"Hey, it's the last day! Wanted to come and wish you well." I
didn't get that. It was more the Patrick show. We were in the
Patrick world, and then Ellen came, and there was definitely a
lot of emotion that both of them had individually . . . not necessarily together. It was more so her being there on the day that
he died. He had his own way of being with that, and the same
thing with her. It was like two people who grew up together
and . . . here we are. They had their own way of reflecting.

Patrick Dempsey I very quietly left. It was beautiful. It was
raining, which was really touching. I got in my Panamera, got
in rush-hour traffic, and two hours later I was home.

Big news like this doesn't stay quiet for long. Both Mi-chael Ausiello—who left EW in 2010 to launch the news site TVLine—and Lesley Goldberg of The Hollywood Re-porter *learned two weeks prior to Dempsey's final episode that he would be leaving the show. No reporter worth their salt wants to sit on a scoop—least of all one as huge as this—but Ausiello and Goldberg didn't want to spoil the outcome for fans, so they agreed to hold the story until af-ter the episode aired. I eventually found out, too, but in the nuttiest way imaginable: I was standing on the set of* CSI: Cyber, *watching Patricia Arquette talk about some droll techno-criminal. Unfortunately, the publicist also cc'd Dempsey's manager and ABC publicist while trying to give me a major story, so I couldn't immediately report the scoop. But I did use the information to successfully nego-tiate the one and only exit interview with Dempsey. Two weeks before his final episode, I met him and his publicist at Feed Body & Soul in Venice, California, for a story that would hit newsstands on April 24. He seemed a little shell-shocked and at one point choked up, but at the time he said nothing about how his on-set behavior may have con-tributed to his ouster. My editor, Henry Goldblatt, wanted to put him on the cover of* Entertainment Weekly, *but he couldn't guarantee to ABC that no one would see it before the episode aired. Good thing we didn't: some subscribers got the issue on the morning of Dempsey's final episode—and one actually tweeted the story. Our PR department tried to get the tweets removed, but the cat was out of the bag: some fans found out early that McDreamy was about*

to be McHistory. Outlets like Variety *reported how the story*
got out early, while our PR department released this state-
ment: "We are surprised that an EW subscriber may have
received their issue a day earlier than planned. We always
try our best to bring readers exclusive news first. We would
like to apologize to fans of the show that learned the news
ahead of time." Dempsey's final episode was watched by
8.83 million viewers—the show's largest audience since the
premiere that season. Variety *even pontificated whether the*
ratings boost was due to my exclusive with Dempsey.

Lesley Goldberg (*The Hollywood Reporter*) I'm used to
working with networks to hold news as part of their efforts to
guard against plot spoilers. But the way Patrick Dempsey's exit
was handled involved a layer of paranoia and secrecy that has
been unlike anything I've seen in my reporting career. News
that he was leaving, and his character being killed off, would
have been a major story considering how big the show is do-
mestically and internationally. However, it also would have
meant spoiling the episode and, more important, damaging
key relationships I've worked hard to build. At some point,
publishing the news of Dempsey's exit before the episode
aired became an ethical question of what was more important—a big story and its subsequent traffic, which would have
come no matter what, or the relationships and trust that it
took years to craft. Ultimately, I still published early because
EW subscribers received the issue with Lynette's Dempsey interview before the episode aired.

Mike McColl The morning after Derek's last episode aired, my daughter sent me a link that was on YouTube or Facebook or something. I actually pulled it up to look at it, and it was a *Grey's Anatomy* showbiz cheat sheet. It asked the question "Who is the attending doctor who killed Derek 'McDreamy' Shepherd?" It included a photo that I posted from the set. I had on a bloody rubber glove and was in my scrubs and mask. I never obviously would have posted this before it aired. I posted it well after the episode aired, and I [captioned it] "McDeadly." This writer said something like, "Kill McDeadly." Maybe that's why the producer didn't choose a big-name actor to be the one who killed our beloved McDreamy! I want to be ultrasensitive to these hard-core fans because it means so much to them, and I certainly didn't mean in that case to make light of it. It's just, I'm an actor, and I recognize it for what it is. *Is everybody clear on the fact that this is just pretend and Patrick knew he was going to be leaving the show?* It was just like, "God. He's okay. He really is *okay.*"

Peter Horton Derek was going to be there forever with Meredith because you went through a whole journey with them. That was incredibly fulfilling. So even if he's not there, he's there. I don't think any of us really worried about that going away because by then you were so invested in it. The show can last as it has for years.

Patrick Dempsey Lots of people [miss him]. "It's good to see you alive" is the comment I get. I'm like, "Yes, I'm very much alive in reruns." People were really invested in that relationship. I knew it would be heavy. Very happy to have moved on with a different chapter in my life.

Samantha Sloyan The montage just killed me, when Meredith says, "It's okay, you can go." God, I'm getting choked up just thinking about it. The chemistry they have as a pair and the way they were able to build that and sustain it! So many of these relationships are, like, "Will they, won't they," and then it wears thin. They sustained it for the duration of their relationship on the show, and it's just, I think, a testament to what those two created. It was just unbelievable.

Pompeo addressed Dempsey's departure with a tweet that focused solely on his character, not on how she spent eleven years working side by side with him: "There are so many people out there who have suffered tremendous loss and tragedy. Husbands and wives of soldiers, victims of senseless violence, and parents who have lost children. People who get up every day and do what feels like is the impossible. So it is for these people and in the spirit of resilance [sic] I am honored and excited to tell the story of how Meredith goes on in the face of what feels like the impossible." Meanwhile, fans futilely created a Change.org petition to reinstate McDempsey, while other, more desperate ones simply tweeted "We Hate You" to Rhimes.

Shonda Rhimes Derek Shepherd is and will always be an incredibly important character—for Meredith, for me, and for the fans. I absolutely never imagined saying goodbye to our McDreamy. Patrick Dempsey's performance shaped Derek in a way that I know we both hope became a meaningful example—happy, sad, romantic, painful, and always true—of what young women should demand from modern love. His loss will be felt by all.

Talk about the mother (father?) of all postscripts: In November of 2020 Dempsey reprised his role as McDreamy in the season opener—but only in Meredith's dreams. Stricken with COVID-19, an unconscious Meredith "imagined" reuniting with her husband on the beach. After talking exclusively to Deadline and saying how it was "really a very healing process, and really rewarding," Dempsey would return for more beach-based episodes that would ultimately stand out as the best moments of season seventeen. "It was a second chance thing," one ABC executive told me at the time. "Shonda likes a comeback. Also, they wanted him in their last season."

CHAPTER 9

"It's a Beautiful Day to Save Lives," Or, the Guest Stars Who Survived and Those Who Didn't

Since *Grey's Anatomy* cycles through an endless whiteboard of surgeries and bewildering medical cases, the series was in constant need of dynamic guest stars. Granted, *Grey's* didn't need stunt casting to get eyeballs: Patrick Dempsey and the drama-prone interns (mostly) took care of that. But somebody needed to play the patients who swallowed doll heads, watched porn to manage pain, or became tragically encased in cement. So the casting department, led by the inimitable Linda Lowy, recruited a slew of talented and memorable actors—a great number of whom were relative unknowns who went on to become huge stars.

Sharon Lawrence earned her first Emmy nomination for guest-starring as Izzie's guileless mom, Robbie Stevens, in the season five episode titled "No Good at Saying Sorry (One More Chance)." Robbie visits Izzie after her cancer diagnosis but is never told the whole truth about her daughter for fear it would destroy her.

Sharon Lawrence The world had heard that Izzie came from a hardscrabble background. We were able to construct that her mother was on a different level than Izzie. Robbie was childlike and optimistic about the world rather than someone who was beaten down, based on her circumstances. Robbie didn't mind that she was living in some sort of arrested development. She shows up with a pink headband and a denim skirt that was above the knee, which for a woman that age says a lot, right? And I'm pretty sure I was wearing a candy necklace.

Katie and I had an immediate chemistry. I'd never met her. I didn't really meet her until she was already in the hospital bed with the gear strapped on her. There wasn't a whole lot of chances to hang out in the cast chairs; she was stuck there the whole day. We just locked in right away. By the time I crawled into bed with her, we already knew and trusted each other, and we talked a lot about her mother. She was just in the process of adopting her first child, so mothers meant a lot to her. I've done lots of guest spots on shows, but that one, obviously, had depth to it. That one meant a lot to me.

In season six, Rhimes decided it was time to tell the origin story of Ellis Grey, so she cast Sarah Paulson as a younger (but equally ballsy) version of Meredith's mom in the season six episode "The Time Warp." There was a lot of action packed into those forty-four minutes: we met her young husband, Thatcher (John Ainsworth), and her young lover, Dr. Richard Webber (J. August Richards), while she dealt with sexism at Seattle Grace and treated a patient with "gay-related immune deficiency"—otherwise known as AIDS.

Sarah Paulson I remember thinking, You want me to play Meredith's mother? I have brown eyes and Kate has blue eyes. Everybody is going to know that! The truth of the matter was, I was not working at all. It was a very big acting opportunity for me. I took it very seriously, because I knew how beloved the character was. I really wanted to get it right. The episode dealt with AIDS! Leave it to *Grey's Anatomy.* They never shy away from that kind of thing. That's one of the more remarkable things about the show, is they tackle all of these important topics, everything from social and racial injustice to health crises of all kinds. But it's always character driven. I feel very honored to be part of the history of that show.

Hilarie Burton played a craniofacial surgeon who had a quickie with Dr. Arizona Robbins (Jessica Capshaw) in season nine before leaving the show after three episodes. Her husband, Jeffrey Dean Morgan, played Denny in seasons two and five, but the couple didn't start dating until 2009 (they married ten years later). That alone made her a source of fascination (or resentment) among the fans.

Hilarie Burton (Dr. Lauren Boswell) I had no idea who Jeffrey was [when we began dating]. I'd been working nonstop since I was twenty, twelve- to eighteen-hour days, every single day. I wasn't watching television. I had no idea what was going on in the real world. So when I was introduced to him by [*Supernatural* actor] Jensen Ackles and his wife, Danneel, they made an offhand remark, like, "Oh, this is our buddy. We want to set you up with him. He just did an action movie."

So that first night we met, I made fun of him. Then I called a friend of mine from high school and said, "I just kissed a guy who's like an action hero." My friend was like, "You kissed Denny!" He flipped out. He was the one who alerted me to the Denny of it all. Then my brother, [who] was in a punk band and covered in tattoos, was like, "You kissed Denny!" It was men who were telling me what a big deal he was. Both men and women love Jeffrey. That's what I've learned.

I was there [as Lauren] to cause trouble. They were, like, "We want you to come in and break up this beloved lesbian couple." That was very scary, but they were like, "We need someone who people feel like is the girl next door." So that's not as threatening as some family member coming in. I mean, they could have hired some busty sexy lady to come in and instead they hired that awkward girl next door.

Fans *hated* me. When it aired, I went to dinner with my husband and I saw these two ladies who looked at me with so much disdain. Jeffrey was like, "They've seen [your episodes]." I remember doing press for it and was really trying to temper the seriousness of the situation with good humor. All of my interviews at the time were like, "I'm here for trouble." I will still get comments on Instagram. I posted something about my book the other day and someone sent me a message that said, "How could you break up Callie and Arizona?" I wrote back, "It was easy and fun."

In seasons eleven and fourteen, Geena Davis (Thelma & Louise) appeared as Dr. Nicole Herman, the head of fetal surgery at Grey Sloan who went blind after surgery to remove her brain tumor.

Geena Davis I get a lot of in-person reaction to that role. It's so interesting. It used to be that a teen who would meet me for the first time would say they recognized me from *A League of Their Own*. Now, teens recognize me from *Grey's Anatomy*. It's almost guaranteed that a teen boy or a girl is going to say, "Are you Dr. Herman?"

Matthew Morrison was absolutely beloved as Glee's Will Schuester, the man who turned the William McKinley High School glee club into a show choir to watch on the competition circuit. So when it was announced in season thirteen that he was cast as Dr. Paul Stadler, the estranged and abusive ex-husband of Jo (Camilla Luddington), the reaction was one of shock and disbelief. Schue as a wifebeater?! But that was exactly the kind of role that Morrison had been looking for.

Matthew Morrison It was such a dream part for me. When you do a show like *Glee* for so long, you kind of want to shake off that character and have people see you in a new light. So this was a beautiful opportunity. I really wanted to go the opposite way of who you would think this guy is. A lot of people, I think, would go in and play that harsh and mean, mustache-twirling kind of villainous character. I wanted to go completely opposite and be the most charming person you could possibly meet. I think everyone has dual personalities, but we are surrounded by so many people in this world who put on such a great front. That person could be your best friend, but they have a dark side that you just would never know. That's really what I wanted to bring to this character.

It was amazing working with Camilla. The whole time we were filming, she would not sit next to me. I remember a few times when I would just kind of fuck with her and invade her space a little bit. She would laugh it off, but she was really kind of freaked out by me. She needed to have her space from me, and I really respected that. It was four episodes that I got to be on. I think they were really excited about my performance, but they kind of wrote themselves into a corner by killing my character. They were, like, "Oh God, we just want to keep you on." It's just one of those television moments, like, "Let's wrap this thing up and put a nice clean bow on it." I think it had a lot of power, and if we would have drawn it out any more, it might have lost some of that impact. So it was perfect.

[Afterward] I did a show called *The Greatest Dancer* in the U.K. and one of my costars was so scared of me. She was just so taken aback by [Stadler] that she thought there must be something like that in me because he's so evil. I take it as a compliment when people are scared.

Camilla Luddington (Dr. Jo Wilson) Paul had been such a huge presence in Jo's life for so long, so when they finally ran into each other . . . I will forever remember shooting that scene, feeling anxious about doing it because it was such a huge moment for Jo's story line. I stayed away from Matthew off camera, which sucks because he's so nice. I would've loved to get to know him more. But I knew that we had to have a certain chemistry, and I didn't want to become too familiar with him. Staying away helped me to hate him. He was so great at playing a charismatic bad guy.

Viewers learned very early in the show's run that Derek had four sisters—but it took years to meet them all. Nancy Shepherd (Embeth Davidtz) was introduced in season two, followed by Amelia Shepherd (Caterina Scorsone) in season seven, Liz Shepherd (Neve Campbell) in season nine, and Kathleen Shepherd (Amy Acker) in season fifteen, when all four ladies and their mom, Carolyn (Tyne Daly, who first appeared in season five) came together for an epic dinner.

Embeth Davidtz I actually had just discovered the show when they asked me to do that part, so I was excited to meet everyone. It was really at the height of the show's success. Patrick was especially warm and lovely. We have a mutual friend in Amy Adams, and he had just shot *Enchanted* with her, so we had some fun and fond stories to share about Amy's quirkiness.

What I do recall very clearly is how fast they shot. My head was spinning. I had not really done much TV, and they have a super-ambitious schedule, so we moved at a crazy pace and I felt like a bit of a slow klutz trying to keep up with all of them.

[For the dinner scene in season fifteen,] it was blocked and shot very much like a play. We did long takes and that was fun, lots of double entendres. Comedy of error–ish moments are always more fun to shoot than small bits of a scene at a time. We were on location in one of those huge old houses in Hancock Park [a historic residential neighborhood in L.A.] and we had a great upstairs room that all the actors would retire to between scenes and compare outrageous war stories from being in the business.

Amy Acker There were a couple of times we tried to work out different guest spots to do on the show, and it just hadn't worked out. Then I got a call. They asked, "Do you want to play one of the Shepherd sisters?" And I was like, "Oh, I'm glad none of those other things worked out!" It worked out.

Shooting the dinner scene . . . first of all, Embeth is, like, I just want to *be* her. And Caterina is so sweet, and after being on a show for that long, just has a positive attitude and such a strong work ethic. And then Tyne coming in! It's like everything stops when she's there because everyone is in awe. She comes in, does her thing, and it's like this beautiful whirlwind of a performance. I left thinking how I wish there was just a Shepherd family spin-off, because I'd like to work with them all again.

Mousey, Weirdo, and Circus Act may not have been the most affectionate terms of endearment for the character of Heather

Brooks, but Tina Majorino relished the aspect of playing the peculiar surgical intern in seasons nine and ten—especially the part where she jumped into bed with Justin Chambers on her first day of work.

Tina Majorino I had no idea that was going to happen, because the script was top secret. I went into my trailer to get dressed and there were only undergarments. So at seven in the morning, I met Justin, we were in our robes, and it went from the cordial hellos to me straddling him, with the wardrobe ladies arranging the sheets around us. I think in some ways it was good I didn't know, because I didn't have time to worry or overthink it. Justin is a really sweet dude.

Heather's a very present, very open woman. I think she follows her joy and goes for what she wants. If it works out, great; if it doesn't, it doesn't. She's in a constant flow state. It's admirable. To me, she always seemed like the kind of female friend I would want, someone who would encourage you to own who you are, to be okay with your sexuality and how you express it and who you express it with. She's not someone who leads with shame or buys into it. And she doesn't dish it out, either. Live and let live. I love that about her. So, to me it made sense [to sleep with Karev].

I was known as the Butterfinger Bandit on set. I don't know how, but I subsisted on mainly Butterfingers and coffee that entire season. It was absurd, and it was a "thing." I ate them all. It was such a thing that on my last day, Gaius [Dr. Shane Ross] made an amazing speech and led the crew in a Butterfingers cheer for my send-off. It made me cry, it was really sweet.

The name Mike McColl—or the character he played, Dr. Paul Castello—might not ring a bell for most fans. But if you see his face, chances are good you'll recognize him instantly: he was the doctor who killed Derek in season eleven because he wouldn't do a CT scan of his brain. In a genius bit of guest casting for the show's 350th episode, the show brought McColl back to play a member of the medical board that was deciding Meredith's future as a doctor. In a final act of comeuppance for Derek, Dr. Castello has a seizure at one of the hearings and dies on Dr. Tom Koracick's operating table.

Mike McColl I was actually working on *Shameless*, and my agents emailed me saying that *Grey's* wanted me back. The idea was to bring me back as the panel chair, which was obviously a very powerful choice. Ellen was so awesome. It was a very nice reunion. There were some pointed jokes at old Dr. Castello, that's for sure. But she's a total sweetheart. It was really cool to get to work with her a second time around and to have another great interaction with her. [For the seizure] I actually went down pretty hard. Everybody's around me and I foam at the mouth and stuff. That was a bit of a workout to get that. After the episode aired, everybody was pretty much like, "Hated to see you die, but you kind of had it coming."

In season sixteen, up-and-coming actress Beanie Feldstein (Booksmart) had her dreams come true when she played Tess Anderson, a cancer patient who disguises herself as a bright intern who garners the attention of Dr. Richard Webber.

Beanie Feldstein I. Am. The. Biggest. Fan. I had been chatting back and forth with the incredible Finchie [writer/producer Elisabeth R. Finch] on Instagram, and I also told my agents, "If *Grey's Anatomy* would ever let me on their set for any reason, the answer is yes!" I'm such a big fan that when I was on the set, they took me into this room where they keep all the prosthetic heads of every actor who has played a character they have had to perform facial or brain surgery on. And they said, "Okay, guess!" I got every single one right. I thrived! I was, like, "Jane Doe played by Elizabeth Reaser! Caroline Aaron when she was the woman with tongue cancer! Henry . . . ooh, Henry, my heart can't take it, I have to love away!" Both Linda Klein and Meg Marinis, who directed and wrote the episode I was lucky enough to be in, were honestly disturbed by my knowledge. Like, I cut too deep.

[Walking onto the set] was completely and utterly surreal. It was like stepping into a world I knew like the back of my hand, and yet at the same time felt totally different. I toured every last corner. The crew was so remarkably kind to me. If I had a little break, someone would come up to me with big eyes and say, "Do you want to see Mer's kitchen? Do you want to hold the Post-it? Do you want to go in the OR gallery?" I was in *heaven*. I didn't keep the stethoscope [that Webber gave me in the episode]. However, the props department was so giving and they made a swag bag that they sent me home with. I have a *Grey's Anatomy* mug and pen and bag! And my favorite is that they recycle all of the old scripts to create notepads, so I now write exclusively on notepads that on the back have the words of Callie and Cristina and Arizona.

Oh, and I'm a Denny girl. Always and forever. But mostly, I'm a Cristina girl.

Though her character of Ellis Grey died in season three, Kate Burton became the Very Special Guest Star of Grey's Anatomy *because her ghost kept coming back. Every time she'd appear in a posthumous episode—be it "Some Kind of Miracle" or "Blood and Water"—she'd get the guest star of distinction at the beginning of the episode.*

Kate Burton Shooting the pilot was quick and so fast, I literally thought, I will never see any of these people ever again. It was just that one time. I've always been a realist as an actor. I just thought, It's unlikely that I'll see any of these people ever again. And so here we are and I am about to do an episode of *Grey's Anatomy* [sixteen years later]. I come on about two to three times a year as a ghost, a vision, a nightmare, as a person walking through the hall, as an image. I'm always in Ellen's head. There were many ghost sightings of Ellis Grey. Then for five years, they apparently talked about me all the time, but of course I was not in it. Why would I be? Because I was not alive.

Many things have just been offered to me because of Ellis Grey. I was nominated for two Emmys for playing Ellis Grey . . . my first time being nominated. And then I joined *Scandal* and I got another Emmy nomination. I was like, "Shonda, what else have you got for me? Do you have other things you are writing for me that I'm going to get nominated for?" I'm just teasing. It's such an honor to be nominated because you can't believe your characters have that kind of indelible impact. That's Shonda.

I really do feel like there's a whole group of us, we're in her repertory company, and I'm a charter member. So is Jeff Perry. There's a little group of us who have done her shows. You sit in those rooms to do those table reads—it's really kind of a dingy room—and you're with Shonda, Betsy, the great directors, the great cinematographers, the great cast and crew, and you're like, There's nowhere else I'd rather be.

CHAPTER 10

"Somebody Sedate Me," Or, How *Grey's Anatomy* Managed to Gross You Out

Fans may like to spend hours opining over who should sleep with whom when the characters are off rounds—but that doesn't mean the medical cases took a back seat to all that great sex and romance. Nothing has been more entertaining than watching the cast cut, carve, and chisel their way into prosthetic bodies over the last two decades. And keeping that up was a monumental task for the cast and crew.

Justin Chambers Real doctors do not have this many amazing cases. But we need to be appointment television every week.

Mark Saul I would go through *The Seattle Times* and look for interesting Seattle-related medical issues or emergency situations. I would look at medical journals, too. They wanted it to be realistic and all based on something that really happened.

Matt Mania When we [the crew] would make a comment about something, it would be something more like, "Wow, that could never happen," as far as the medical situation. I remember [medical adviser technician] Linda Klein and how she would just be rolling her eyes and pulling her hair out because some of the stuff they would have them do medically just was so out of the norm and not realistic sometimes. She would desperately try to make sure there was some medical integrity about the whole thing. I think she would end up getting her way quite a bit. There was a Siamese twin one where they separated them in, like, a day.

Harry Werksman ABC said, "You can tell whatever medical story you want, but there has to have been at least one recorded case of it." I was the one who gave the staff syphilis. I just happened to have read, prior to writing the episode, about an outbreak of syphilis among the staff at a hospital in New Hampshire. It happened exactly the way we did it on the show, where there was a nurse who was sleeping with doctors. It sort of spoke to the whole thing how there's a lot of sex happening in the hospital, in the on-call rooms, in empty patient rooms, in stairwells. They're working eighty, ninety, one hundred hours a week. They have no time off to do these kinds of shenanigans.

Eric Buchman In a weird way, a show that was a thorn in our heels was *House,* because that had just premiered on Fox and was a huge hit medical show that really played up the medical mystery. It was considered a serious medical show, and my job, of course, was to watch every *House* episode to make sure we weren't doing what they're doing. But I remember on a network level, them saying our show wasn't *House*-y enough. So we were getting notes saying, "Do more of a medical mystery." But of course, Shonda being Shonda, she knew what the tone of her show was.

Rob Corn I'm always one to push the envelope toward more gore, especially in our surgical scenes. I went too far a bunch of times but always provided a way to cut away if necessary. I loved showing the details of surgeries, much to a lot of people's chagrin.

Robert Baker When we would get the scripts for the table reads, all the medical stuff would just be the word "medical." So you'd be reading the script and it would be like, "We've got to medical the medical until medical happens to medical." Like, that would be the table read. The surgery scenes were just like Mad Libs but inserting the word "medical" in everything. Eventually one of the drafts would have all the medical terminology in it.

Patrick Dempsey There was this one word, something to do with a blood clot in the spine, and I just could not figure out how to say it. I kept going, "Can I just say, 'It's not looking so good,' and then cut to a commercial?"

Giacomo Gianniotti (Dr. Andrew DeLuca) My first surgery was a nightmare. There were so many things, general rules that I didn't know about sterilization, keeping everything clean. I was constantly dropping my hands in surgery and Linda Klein would be like, "Cut, cut, cut! Giacomo, what are you doing? You're dropping your hands! You're not sterile!"

Kelly McCreary People study a long time to be surgeons. We get ten minutes.

Tina Majorino Surgery scenes were always my favorite. I'm someone who absolutely loves to work with fake blood and fake injuries and all that fun gore stuff. I am not squeamish. *However,* one day we had to shoot a scene where we were operating on a patient who had trichotillomania. She had eaten her hair and it formed a tumorlike ball in her stomach. I didn't think anything of it until we went to shoot. They used an animal stomach and made this hair ball and it's covered in all the fake goop and blood. It was awesome. While I'm not squeamish, I *do* have a weird thing with hair. Clumps of hair freak me out. Like, drain hair? Forget it. So the more takes we're doing, the more I feel like I'm going to pass out. I just went white. I remember Ellen looked at me at one point, and I don't know how she knew with most of my face covered, but she just grabbed both my hands and said, "Okay, and we're breathing. We're breathing. Deep breaths through the nose. Let it out. You got this." It makes me laugh my ass off now, thinking about all of the other textbook stomach-turning stuff I saw during my time on that show that I had no issue with. But the hair ball did me in a little.

Brooke Smith I was so into it when we were doing surgeries. Whenever my husband and I would see a car accident I'd be like, "Maybe we should stop and I can help someone." He was like, "No, you've been playing a doctor on TV for like two weeks. Calm down."

Choreographing the surgeries was left to a terrific group of experts who became celebrities in their own right, thanks to the show. Besides Klein, who also played Nurse Linda in the OR, there was Tom and Bari Burman on prosthetics and special effects and Norman T. Leavitt on the wound makeup. Dr. Zoanne Clack has served as a long-term consultant and writer on the show.

Harry Werksman There's a steep learning curve. You can sit in the writers' room and be like, "Oh, we're going do a craniotomy," but now we have to build a fake skull to pop off. We have to be accurate about the instrumentation that we're using and how they do it. There was a lot of prep that went into stuff that would maybe be a minute, two minutes, on-screen. As time went on, we just got better at it, but it's like the first time after Addison showed up, and we started to need babies on the show because that was her specialty. You can get small children, but sometimes you need them even smaller. There was an episode with quintuplets or sextuplets, a whole conveyor belt delivery scene that we did. Those were animatronic, those babies. They had to be small. That took forever to shoot that scene. It's four minutes at the end of the episode that took two days to shoot. That was a real example of what a ballet it had to be in terms of getting the surgeries right.

Tom Burman Babies are the hardest thing that we've ever made. The problem is they don't generally have any character. They're kind of a nebulous form and pudgy, and they don't have muscle structure, bone structure, or anything. Because they're so brand new in this world, they don't have all the flaws and things that allow you to use sometimes as cover or identification. And you can't use regular human hair because babies have real fine hair. You have to use animal hair or a type of wool. Angora, so it's real fine. Otherwise, the follicles of hair coming out of the skin in a big close-up look like they were punched in. Each one of those hairs are put in individually and they have to be really fine and wispy.

Norman Leavitt Linda Klein would have this great morgue of bones . . . arm bones, face bones. She could make up a bone sticking out of a shirt. They would cut a shirt away and she would rig this broken bone with meat around it and blood and paste, and it would make you want to throw up. It looked so real. For a long time, she used real flank steak for things. For close-ups, it had to show a horrible wound, a bone sticking through meat.

Jason George (Dr. Ben Warren) Scott Foley was on the show years ago [as Henry Burton], so there's a molding of his head that is often used to sub in when they don't have an actor on the operating table.

Zoanne Clack It's a total puzzle. There are so many things where I just want to say, "No, that can't work." The writers don't know medicine, necessarily. I mean, they know a lot about it now. But they don't know the boundaries, whereas I immediately know the boundaries, so it's always me having to let go of them. We go to experts who are immediately like, "No, that cannot happen." Then we're like, "What if this and this happened?" Then we can have a conversation and a lot of times, they're like, "I guess it could, but it would be extremely rare." We're like, "Yes! That's what we're looking for!" We are the one percent hospital.

And those one percent cases will remain forever ingrained in the heads of fans—if not the guest actors who participated in them. Take James Immekus, for example, who thought he was joining the season four finale to play a dumb kid who jumps off the roof of his house in hopes of hitting the pool— but doesn't. Turns out the producers had something much more heavy in mind for him for "Freedom" parts one and two—his character jumps into a tub of cement.

James Immekus (Andrew Langston) I think it was probably for NDA purposes that the audition was for a kid who jumps off the roof and misses the pool. It kind of had the same intentions, like he did it to impress a girl. Once I booked it, they were like, "Well, that's not what's happening to you. And you have a makeup session coming up and you're going to be fitted for this rock." I had no idea whatsoever.

Zoanne Clack That came from the mind of Shonda Rhimes. That was one that actually took a long time to research, because it doesn't really happen. We were trying to figure out the effect cement has on the body. The main point of that was to get all of our characters together. We're like, "What about something like 'Cement Boy,' where we can get everyone together?" There were different stories that came off of it, but that was the main story of the episode.

James Immekus When I got to the Burman Studio for the first time, they had this chair that was already encased in a rock. I guess it was all plaster and, just like you see in the show, they wanted to be able to pull it off in pieces. It would take about an hour to seal me in. I got there at four in the morning for two weeks straight. It's like I lost a bet or something. I was legitimately sealed in the rock. People would offer me water and I was like, "No. No water." There was no catheter. I just made sure I didn't take anything until it was lunchtime [since] I would be in it for a couple of hours. It wasn't the worst thing. But there were some situations where I could feel my legs falling asleep. The cast was really wonderful to work with. Sandra Oh, Sara Ramirez, they would massage my hands and legs for me between takes. It was pretty nice of them. The experience in and of itself was not bad. It was just, obviously, having to sit in one place for quite a while.

Breaking the character out of his cement tomb also gave the writers a chance to show off a lovable side of Bailey. After Cement Boy starts to feels sorry for himself and calls himself a loser, Bailey gives a speech about how Han Solo, who was encased in carbonite in Star Wars: Episode V—The Empire Strikes Back, *is remembered for making "the Kessel run in less than twelve parsecs and who braved the subzero temperatures of the ice planet Hoth in order to save someone he cared about from the big ugly wampa. He's remembered as the guy who swooped down at the last minute, blasted Darth Vader out of the sky so that Luke could use the Force and destroy the damn Death Star. Princess Leia saved him from the carbonite. They fell in love, they saved the universe, and had twin Jedi babies that went on to save the universe again, right? That's the whole picture. The carbonite was just a piece."*

Zoanne Clack It was fun because we found out facts about Bailey and her sci-fi nerdiness. There were certain things we were able to learn from them working together that was strictly from the minds of the writers and trying to make it work within the realm of reality.

But just as Star Wars *fans will never forget how Darth Vader encased Han Solo in carbonite,* Grey's *fans will never forget Cement Boy.*

James Immekus I was at a wedding in Georgia once and I had some server at the wedding say, "This girl is losing her mind. Would you go over and say hi to her?" So I went over and she said, "It's crazy to meet Cement Boy!" I guess it got circulated on the internet that I'm Cement Boy. So, yeah.

In the season two episode titled "Something to Talk About," Joseph Sikora played a sensitive father-to-be named Shane who's treated like a circus attraction because of his "hysterical pregnancy." In reality, Shane is carrying a teratoma, a rare (and pretty heinous) tumor that develops tissue, hair, and teeth. Sikora went on to play drug dealer Tommy Egan on Starz's *hit crime drama* Power.

Zoanne Clack I was *really* excited about that one. One of the big learning curves I had to make was trying to open up my mind and not say no all the time in the first couple of seasons. This was one of the ones where my initial thought was, Are you kidding me? We can't do this. But then I realized that a teratoma puts out hormones that you make during pregnancy. Things like liver disease will make your belly really bloated, because it's filled with fluid, but there's nothing that would give the positive pregnancy test. When I found that, I was ecstatic. That was a major coup, a major feature in my hat to figure out how to actually make it work medically.

Joseph Sikora (Shane Herman) I did read for the role. I was very grateful that Linda Lowry cast me. She made me very comfortable—I'm a nervous wreck at auditions—and even explained that the sides were written in a bit of code because they didn't want the gag of the man mistakenly thinking he was pregnant to get out. Instead of saying, "I'm pregnant," in the audition they had the character saying, "I'm a duck." I just tried to play the truth of the situation as best I could. Alie Ward, who played my wife, was fantastic. I really appreciated her. She made it easy to pretend I had a loving partner. The prosthetics weren't too bad during the course of the shoot, but getting the belly and chest piece made was an interesting process. They made a body cast of me from shoulders to hips, and from what I remember I lost some skin from my nipple when they pulled off the plaster cast. But they very wisely made a kind of shirt that I just had to slip on every day. It was incredibly hot! But not too uncomfortable. And even if it was, I was just happy to be working. I'm not big into complaining.

Complaining was the furthest thing from Sunkrish Bala's mind when he scored a guest gig in the season two episode "Much Too Much." He was still in college and had done only "two tiny gigs" before that and was "brand new to the business." Like Immekus and Sikora, Bala didn't get the full story when he was hired. Initially, he thought he was playing a man with brain cancer. Instead, he got the role of a man who has a one-night stand with Meredith and never loses his erection, a condition known as priapism.

Sunkrish Bala (Steve Murphy) The note from the casting director was to "lean into the comedy." It was confusing. I remember the designer asking me to put a hairbrush in my pants during a wardrobe fitting because I think the wardrobe department wasn't sure how much they were going to show on-screen. But I think that idea was quickly nixed.

Harry Werksman I was inspired by the Viagra ads that said, "If you have an erection lasting longer than four hours, seek immediate medical attention." So I was like, "Well, what if he didn't take Viagra and this was happening. What would the problem be?" And it turned out to be a spinal tumor that put pressure on certain nerves. There was Meredith having to deal with her one-night stand who had this problem, and of course it ended up that it was Derek's case, so he had to perform the surgery on the tumor that Meredith scrubbed in on. So there were Derek and Meredith, having broken up and her having a one-night stand with the permanent boner.

Sunkrish Bala I had no idea what walking into a hit show would be like. I distinctly remember walking into the makeup trailer and everyone was raucously passing around an interview Katherine had done with a big magazine and discussing it animatedly. At lunch, Ellen told a couple of us how she had gotten *Punk'd* by Ashton Kutcher the previous weekend. I had arrived

on another planet. I was so unprepared for the attention broken penis guy would receive. It was before cable exploded, and
Grey's was just one of those shows that *everyone* watched. It
aired over Thanksgiving weekend that year, and on my South-
west flight back to college that Sunday, people kept coming by
my seat to take photos. To this day it is the role I'm probably
most called out on the street for. Sometimes it's, "Hey, were you
on *Grey's Anatomy* a long time ago?" And sometimes it's, "Hey,
you're the broken penis guy!"

*Leave it to Shonda Rhimes to make porn viewing a medical
necessity. In the episode "Bring the Pain" from season two,
Henry Lamott (the late Brent Briscoe) uses an X-rated flick
called* Nasty Naughty Nurses 4 *to help ease the pain from a
herniated disk, since he's allergic to all pain medication. But
when power goes out in the hospital, Cristina has to step in
and talk dirty to Henry to help keep his endorphins flowing.*

Zoanne Clack That one was kind of a last-minute inclu-
sion, if I remember correctly. We were talking about how we
really wanted Derek to be a pain management doctor, which
is so apropos. We realized that there are certain hormones and
things that are released when you watch porn. Cristina's so
wrapped up in it, it gave her this moment to be [present and
think], I can see how this works scientifically, so now I'm going
to try and work with it.

Mark Tinker We all sort of got our laughs and any discom-
fiture out during rehearsal and when we were shooting. Both
Sandra and [Brent] were very professional. And I behaved well

for a change. Sometimes those scenes can head south where everyone gets the giggles, but as I recall we all did fine and shot it without incident.

Oh, doll: Why do you like to swallow doll heads? In "Enough Is Enough," from the same season, Meredith thought Mr. Hubble (Scott Michael Campbell) was acting as a mule for a drug dealer. In reality, he was just a disturbed young man who swallowed the heads of ten Judy dolls.

Zoanne Clack We thought about a guy swallowing something, and then we really wanted something that would stand out on X-ray. I want to say there was a case where someone swallowed Barbie doll heads, but we couldn't use the name "Barbie," so we named them Judy dolls. Basically, we were just researching all different kinds of ingestions that people did and we wanted it to be something that wouldn't kill them right away. A lot of people swallow paper clips and knives, which we did later with the prisoner, because they do that a lot.

Faith Prince and Arye Gross were cast as a divorced couple who couldn't pull themselves apart—quite literally. In the season three episode titled "Oh, the Guilt," Prince's character has an IUD that got caught on her ex's pierced penis.

Zoanne Clack That was literally like, "Are we able to do that theoretically?" I had to go figure out how that could be possible, even if it didn't actually happen. It's like, "How do we make this work for the story we want to tell?"

Faith Prince (Sonya Cowlman) When I first got the call from my agent, he goes, "Are you sitting down?" That's the way it started. I said, "No, should I be?" And he goes, "Yes, go find somewhere to sit." And then he told me they wanted me to do this episode, and then I thought, Oh my God, they've seen me on *Huff*, because I did this weird, bizarre role on it for Showtime. It was all sex and drugs; they had me in a leopard G-string. I'm guessing they saw me in that and thought, This is our girl. I was going be the weird person doing all of these weird situations! I said to my agent, "Well, okay, it sounds kind of bizarre and funny. I'm in." They made [Arye and me] put this weird pillow between the two of us, and after a while he and I were just like, "Fuck it." It was so uncomfortable, and it was the weirdest angle. I remember thinking how it was sort of Olympic in a way, getting through it. I don't think I've ever seen the episode. My son was going to Laurel Hall in the San Fernando Valley at the time, and I thought, God, I hope the mothers don't see this. It might be the talk of the PTA. I don't think my son has ever seen it. He's twenty-five now. He probably never has to.

Mitch Pileggi (Lawrence Jennings) may have played the chairman of the hospital board at Seattle Grace, but even he got a turn playing a patient in the season three episode titled "Desire." While skinny-dipping in the Amazon River, a parasite made its way into Larry's urethra. Ewwww.

Zoanne Clack We can't make that up! It happens. The fish will follow the stream of urine into the penis, and this was a

case I think we read about in season one or two and literally
tried to put it in three or four episodes. It would always fall out
or it didn't work in the episode or we had too much story and
we had to let go of one. We finally accomplished it. It was Mark
Wilding who put it in the episode and made it work.

*Dr. Owen Hunt introduces a novel way for the residents to
practice their surgical techniques—cutting up pigs in the season five episode dubbed "Life During Wartime."*

Mark Wilding I don't know that they do it anymore, but to
help train doctors in the field, they would go and stab pigs. I
mentioned that idea and Shonda loved it . . . the idea that Dr.
Owen Hunt walked everybody through how to kill pigs and
how it would make you a better surgeon. We didn't use real
pigs. We got some pigs that were made. We just showed a bunch
of pigs being stabbed. It was very interesting, because ABC ap-
proved the story. But when they actually saw it, which was only
two days before it was supposed to air, they decided it was too
gory, so we had to go back in and essentially redo it to make it
look much *less* gory. We took out some of the blood spurts. I
thought I was going to catch holy hell from People for the Ethical Treatment of Animals, but there was a speech in the episode
by Izzie, who said how appalled she was by what they were
doing. PETA ended up sending me a bunch of flowers and then
I won something called the Genesis Award from some pro-
animal organization. It was by default that I won that, because
I didn't really necessarily agree with the message.

Lexie Grey reacted like all of us (with a bloodcurdling scream) when Jerry Adams (Art Chudabala) stepped out of a car with tree branches for hands in this season seven episode titled "Superfreak." Mark Sloan (Eric Dane) took the lead on the case, while Lexie was ordered by Bailey to stay with Jerry, who had contracted a rare HPV virus that gave him grotesque warts and, well, tree hands. Like the real case in India, he was dubbed "the Tree Man."

Zoanne Clack It was based on a little boy from somewhere in Central America. There are videos about him going to get it treated in India or something, and then he went back home and his [tree hands] grew back again. We talked to a bunch of experts about it. It was really interesting because I was like, "I don't even understand how warts turn into that." There was a lot of research, but we also were trying to figure out how this could happen in America because the little boy it happened to was from this little remote village on some island or something. So we had to base our premise on a backstory.

Art Chudabala One advantage I had was that I had auditioned for a similar role for an episode of *Nip/Tuck*. I guess I had some past experience to draw from! I had an idea of what this man would feel based on other cases that I found in Indonesia. I saw a lot of pictures. You wouldn't think it would be like what you saw on *Grey's*. Like, you would think, Wow, there's no such thing. But it's actually much worse. The feet, the nails would grow into little tree trunks. My makeup was a two-step process. We did the mask and all the latex stuff so they could make actual prosthetics. The makeup took maybe six hours to apply.

They did all those warts by hand. It had taken so long that I remember after the first day of shooting, I decided that I was just going to leave it on for the night. I went home all warted up. It kind of helped with the acting, the sense of discomfort. I had done a bunch of play readings with Sandra Oh before, with the East West Players. I walked up to her in full makeup and was like, "Hey, what's up, Sandra?" She did a full-on gasp and didn't recognize me. Another funny thing I remember was Shonda Rhimes just walking down the hall. She spotted me as I came up and said, "Oh my God, you look great," and walked away. I was like, "Okay, here we go."

"Not Everyone Has to Be Happy All the Time. That Isn't Mental Health. That's Crap," Or, Eleven of the Most Memorable Episodes of *Grey's Anatomy*

After sixteen seasons and 350-plus episodes, characters and surgeries start to blend together. Even Ellen Pompeo has admitted on Twitter that her fans remember more about her character than she does. But a handful of episodes will always remain unforgettable—even the truly odd ones.

"Into You Like a Train"
Season Two, Episode Six
Written by Krista Vernoff
Directed by Jeff Melman

Vernoff received her first Emmy nomination for writing,

while Melman was recognized by the Directors Guild of America for the episode about a pair of train wreck victims who were impaled together on a pole. It not only showcased the impressive work by special effects man Tom Burman, it gave the guest actors/victims—Monica Keena as Bonnie and Bruce A. Young as Tom—the opportunity to actually outshine the regular stars.

Jeff Melman Initially it was pretty overwhelming in terms of the prep. I remember our medical meetings were very long, to make sure we were going down the right path in terms of two people getting impaled by a pole. I sort of approached it, you know, like you would eating an elephant: one bite at a time. We had to figure out how they were going to be face-to-face on a gurney. We also had to make sure that the audience understood that the organs and blood vessels were cauterized, so there was no bleeding. Everybody wants to make sure that it looks real, though I never necessarily heard of another incident like it. But all the doctors agreed that it *could* happen.

Zoanne Clack That was absolutely fabricated. We talked about impalements, and it's funny because we usually have one big impalement a season. This was obviously one of the first and the biggest. We had a demonstration where people would sit together to figure out how they would fit together. In the writers' room, our married writing team [Tony Phelan and Joan Rater] became our models. They got together so I could see where the pole could go and what organs it would go through and how it could affect them but still have them talking. We called them Bonnie and Clyde. One ended up being called Bonnie, but we changed the other one. There's a lot of placement names that we have in the writers' room that don't quite make it to screen.

Monica Keena My two audition scenes were the one where Bruce and I are first wheeled into the ER and the one right before we go into surgery before I ultimately end up dying—and I know I'm going to die. The subject was obviously unavoidable, but at that time I was unaware of exactly what that would really look like or would entail.

Tom Burman We made a cast of their torsos and stitched them together so we had the right conformity. We made a prosthetic piece that had a fiberglass plate that went around the person, and it attached to one end of the pole. And then the other person would have the same plate and attachment.

Monica Keena The whole getup was really fascinating and took about an hour or more each day to get us in and out of it. And once we were seated on the gurney and attached like that, we really were stuck together to each other all day long! So, yes, Bruce and I got to know each other very well on that weeklong shoot because we were literally forced to spend so much time together. Thankfully, he's a wonderful person and very easy to get along with!

Jeff Melman They don't tell you how to stage it in the script. You come up with that all yourself, and I was really proud of how I had done everything. There was a moment where Meredith is leaning up against a wall, a little hungover. She's still thinking about why Derek didn't immediately choose her. She goes through that monologue, the camera moves in on her, and all the chaos is moving in front of her. Then she said, "This can be the worst thing in my life," and then you reveal the two people impaled on a gurney. She said, "Okay, maybe the second worst."

Monica Keena I'm still recognized from this episode, which is always flattering. I was and am still very proud of my work on that episode, and will always be grateful for having gotten to be a part of such an amazing, iconic show.

"It's the End of the World"/"As We Know It"
Season Two, Episodes Sixteen and Seventeen
Written by Shonda Rhimes
Directed by Peter Horton

It is, literally, the most explosive moment in the history of *Grey's Anatomy*. For the special episode that aired after Super Bowl XL, Meredith removes a projectile from a man's torso and hands it over to bomb squad leader Dylan Young (Kyle Chandler)—who is subsequently blown to smithereens before he even makes it out of the OR.

Shonda Rhimes I remember having to talk it through with [then ABC Entertainment Group president] Stephen McPherson. It was a big deal that we were doing the Super Bowl episode, so I wanted to make sure it was something they wanted to do. He seemed fine with it.

Peter Horton It was a very ambitious proposition. There were a number of long days because of that. When that explosion scene came up, the only way you get through it is with a tremendous amount of prep. We worked on how we wanted to do it, what walls we wanted to collapse, what lights we wanted to fall.

Kyle Chandler The first thing I always remember is the test that was run to simulate the explosion using detonation cord. This was accomplished by taking an ample amount of this explosive to the parking lot of the studio. If I recall correctly, the cord was wrapped around a human-sized dummy, but don't hold me to it. Then . . . everybody back up . . . KAAA-BOOOOM! I could hear car alarms going off as far as Nevada. I assume the amount of det cord used in the actual "pink mist" shot was modulated at that point, as the roof of the studio did not raise on the day.

Shonda Rhimes I always knew the [bomb] moment was going to involve Ellen. I don't know if anyone else was jealous. I don't think anyone thought, like, Oh, great, I want to have *my* hand stuck in a body cavity and stand there with all those horrors.

Ellen Pompeo It was very late at night when we filmed it. I had been working something like seventeen hours. I was exhausted, so I was excited that I didn't have to do the stunt. They had this amazing stunt girl who was going to do it for me. They strapped her to a cable so they could pull her back when Kyle blows up.

Peter Horton The stunt double was fairly young. She wasn't quite prepared for when she got yanked, having landed on her back and getting her head snapped back. And boy, did it. You could hear it. As stunt people do, she immediately sat up and said, "I'm fine." But clearly she had whacked her head hard, so she had to go through concussion protocol. We'd only had one take of this thing, and I needed to have a couple of things adjusted from that one take, so I had Ellen do it.

Ellen Pompeo We had a knock-down, drag-out fight because he insisted I do the stunt. I said, "A fucking professional
stuntwoman just gave herself a concussion doing it. I've been
working eighteen hours. I can barely see straight. Now you want
me to try it?" He was adamant. I was adamant. We were screaming at each other. I even said to him, "Why are you even making
me do this? You're going to use that take with her head bounc-
ing off the floor," because it looked amazing. It was like slow
motion. Anyway, I ended up doing it, despite me not wanting
to. And of course they used the first take.

Peter Horton If you look in the episode, you will see the
stunt girl hit her head. We left that in. It had been very effective.
But we used part of Ellen's take, which is the part she never remembers. We never would have put her in jeopardy. We pulled
her much slower than we pulled the stunt double.

Ellen Pompeo I remember thinking Kyle Chandler was
amazing. I wasn't surprised his career really took off after that,
because he was so natural.

Shonda Rhimes He would pitch me ideas on how Dylan,
his character, could maybe not explode, and I would show him
the line in the script that said, "Dylan explodes." That's literally
all it said. He was written to explode. But I did not expect to
have Kyle Chandler. I didn't want to explode him.

Kyle Chandler I don't remember asking that my character Dylan *not* be killed off, as it was written in the script, but
I wouldn't be worth my salt for not trying to get a recurring
role on the hottest television show airing at the time. For the
life of me, I can't remember if I either begged on my knees or
groveled before Shonda. No matter: Shonda said no. I liked her

immediately when we met. You see, I met Pete Berg on the same lot while working that show during my lunch break one day, and Pete was just starting casting for a new TV show. I think, if not mistaken, Shonda mentioned me to Pete and may have initiated the meeting. The show being cast was titled *Friday Night Lights.* Nothing short of life changing. Of course, there's also an Emmy and a couple nominations involved in the story. Yeah, that was a pretty good gig, all right.

Peter Horton Whenever you direct anything, some of your best moments are accidents. When we did the blast, all of these bits of debris fill the air and come slowly down like a rainstorm. It added such a fabulous texture to that moment, when Ellen is sitting up and looking at the remains of poor Kyle Chandler.

Ellen Pompeo Nothing seemed as monumental back then because we had no idea how long this show would run or how iconic these moments would become.

Peter Horton There were so many moments in the episode. Bailey is having this baby and doesn't know where her husband is, but we know he's been in an accident and he's in another room in the hospital. She's having this baby and we're shooting this shot around her as she's in labor and she's refusing to have the baby because he's not there. Out of nowhere she's, like, yelling in the phone, "Why aren't you there?" Somebody sticks the phone right in the lens, like right up here, and does this emotional raw sort of scream, and it was just not planned. It was just moment after moment like that. It really was the best of *Grey's Anatomy,* because it was the moment the show really went stratospheric in terms of success and popularity.

"Walk on Water"/"Drowning on Dry Land"
Season Three, Episodes Fifteen and Sixteen
Written by Shonda Rhimes
Directed by Rob Corn

Grey's Anatomy went high-tech for this episode about a massive ferry crash in Puget Sound. Since Prospect Studios didn't exactly have a gigantic bay in its back lot, the ferry and water scenes were digitally created by hanging a massive green screen in the parking lot of the Santa Anita racetrack. The episode featured two significant moments: Meredith almost drowned; and Alex ended up falling for one of the victims, a pregnant amnesiac played by Elizabeth Reaser.

Tony Phelan Early on, the studio and the network would come to the read-throughs. They loved that script, so they said to us, "We want to make this a two-parter." We were scheduled to start shooting in, like, two days! Taking an episode and expanding it into two parts while shooting it was a real brainteaser. That was one of those moments when all of us had our laptops open in the writers' room around a big table while passing pages to each other and keeping communication with Rob Corn, who was directing at Santa Anita in the parking lot of the racetrack with these huge green screens.

Norman Leavitt They stacked these cargo containers for the green screen.

Rob Corn We could not take over a ferry landing in Seattle. However, the visual effects were so good, we received calls from the Coast Guard asking where we got the Coast Guard boat. In addition, the morning after it aired, Seattle local news reported that there was a crowd at the ferry launching area looking for remnants of [the show's] crash.

Stacy McKee Some of the water parts we actually shot on our lot in a big, giant tank. Given everything else that her character was going through and just dealing with, it was metaphoric [that Meredith drowned]. She started sinking because there was a moment for her where she didn't mind if she sank.

Derek knew where to retrieve Meredith because a speechless little girl named Lisa pointed to where she had drowned. Off camera, however, Patrick Dempsey didn't make it so easy for the young actress to act heroic.

Madison Leisle (Lisa) I remember Patrick would try to make me laugh the entire time when we were shooting. Like, on camera. He would say, "Don't laugh! Don't laugh! Bet you're gonna laugh!" I was trying to be like so serious, so I would yell, "Why are you doing this to me?"

Meanwhile, the crew was finding it difficult to turn Reaser into an unrecognizable victim.

Norman Leavitt It turns out Elizabeth was very picky and she said she was allergic to everything and couldn't stand glue. Tom Burman was going out of his mind. You hire an actress to play eight weeks of a character, and she can't stand the makeup? We were all looking at each other making sign language like, "What the fuck?" and laughing. That's like hiring a guy to play Frankenstein who doesn't like makeup.

Tom Burman I was so upset. She came in very willing, and then we had to take a cast of her face, and she wanted to know what it was made of, would it hurt her face, she has very sensitive skin and sensitive eyes. Everything we did, what kind of glue we're using, she'd say, "I can't wear that glue. I'm allergic to it." It's all prosthetic and medical adhesives. It's not like we're using some store-bought contact cement or something.

Norman Leavitt Tom went to Rob Corn and said, "We've got to recast her because she can't even take this makeup." Rob says, "Well, there's a problem, because ABC is grooming her for something else. They tried to give her a TV show that didn't make it." So to my horror and Tom's horror, we were told we can't replace her.

Tom Burman We made this prosthetic face for her, but we couldn't glue it down and blend it to the eyes. We had to keep pushing it back down on her face so it wouldn't fall off. They just kept saying, "It'll all work out okay. We'll correct it with CGI if it doesn't work." Well, it looked terrible. The CGI was a really bad job.

No one really noticed, of course. The two-parter ended up averaging more than twenty-five million viewers and was one of the most watched of the season. Reaser would go on to earn a 2007 Emmy nomination for playing Rebecca Pope.

Madison Leisle I had a stand-in and I never wanted to let her work 'cause I just wanted to do it myself. Eventually they just sent her home. People still remember me. I have comments on pictures of mine [on social media] and they ask, "Aren't you the little girl from *Grey's Anatomy*?" and I'm like, "Yep. That's me!"

Tony Phelan It was insane, and the fact that it all cut together was a miracle. We shot it totally out of sequence and did not know what was happening one moment to the next.

"Sanctuary"/"Death and All His Friends"
Season Six, Episodes Twenty-Three and Twenty-Four
Written by Shonda Rhimes
Directed by Stephen Cragg and Rob Corn

In this two-part finale, a gunman who was bereft over the death of his wife returns to Seattle Grace to kill the doctors he believed were responsible for her death: Derek Shepherd, Richard Webber, and Lexie Grey. The episodes featured memorable appearances by Michael O'Neill (shooter Gary Clark) and Mandy Moore (patient Mary Portman), as well as the deaths of surgical residents Reed Adamson (Nora Zehetner) and Charles Percy (Robert Baker). After pitching the finale at the beginning of the season—which had become her routine—Rhimes became racked with self-doubt after she started putting words to the page. "On an almost daily basis, I would come into work and throw myself down on the sofa in the middle of the office and burst into tears like a . . . well, like a bitch baby," she blogged at the time. "I would tell the other *Grey's* writers, 'I don't think I can do this. It's too horrible. People are getting hurt. That man is shooting them.'"

Michael O'Neill It was, literally, the only time I've ever had an executive producer call me at home. Shonda called to talk to me about the role.

Joan Rater Shonda was a giant *West Wing* fan. [O'Neill played Secret Service agent Ron Butterfield on the NBC drama.]

Michael O'Neill I said, "I don't think I can do it. I don't think I have it in me." I had somebody in my family murdered when I was younger, and I know what happens to families when someone gets cut down. You don't really ever recover from it. I talked to my wife, Mary, who said I could do it. So I called Shonda back and said, "I just have to tell you, this frightens me." And she said, "Michael, it frightens me, too." I said that my great fear was that I didn't want it to be sensationalized in a way that we deal with a copycat or any of that. My only requests were that I didn't point a gun at a child and that the character ends his life in the hospital.

Robert Baker It was obviously an intense thing. Without getting involved in the reality of mass shootings in this country, it was not too far out of the realm of imagination. It's something that could happen. It was disturbing, because of how real it is and how real it is to so many people.

Tony Phelan Shonda needed somebody who just felt like this very warm, gregarious, great guy named Gary Clark, so that you understand what he's feeling. Michael and I spent pretty much all of his time on set together when he was doing that episode, and he purposely kept himself away from the other actors because it was such a kind of disturbing story. And he also didn't want to get too comfortable with them. He wanted them to be able to see him in a certain way. In the telling of that story, we took the time to introduce him as a sympathetic character, show the journey that he went through in terms of losing his wife, then have him disappear for a while and then come back.

Michael O'Neill It's the stillness of that character that makes him so dangerous, because you literally don't know where he'll turn next. One of my favorite moments is when I'm on the elevator with Sandra Oh and I ask her where the chief of surgery's office is. She tells me and I say, "Thank you." If she had not told me or had given me attitude, I'd have killed her right there.

Eight minutes into "Sanctuary," Gary shoots Reed in the forehead. Seconds later, he puts a bullet in Karev's torso.

Nora Zehetner I just remember lying in a lot of blood for a really long time. Michael was really lovely. I have two best friends who were obsessed with *The West Wing*, so I had him sign things for them. Being on the other side of it just felt like, you know, I'm going to lay in blood today and I didn't take the heaviness home with me. I've actually never watched that scene. I told my mom not to watch it and then she did and she found it upsetting.

Minutes later, an absentminded April trips over Reed's dead body and falls to the floor. Drenched in Reed's blood, April runs into Derek's office and babbles on about growing up on a farm and how "blood doesn't bother me." Derek puts the hospital on lockdown.

Sarah Drew Putting yourself into that kind of panic mode does something to your body because your body doesn't know that this is *not* happening. I had nightmares and panic attacks while we were shooting that, even for several days after we finished. It was very intense and scary and hard to go to those places, and then leave them at the door and then come home and be like, "I'm fine, I'm fine, nobody's trying to kill me, I didn't just watch my best friend die, I didn't just get covered in her blood."

Rob Corn The director of "Sanctuary," Stephen Cragg, put the ball on the tee for my episode. He did an outstanding job of building the tension throughout. I was grateful for having hit behind him in the batting order. As you can tell, I'm a baseball fan.

Gary claims another victim in the lobby before moving to the floor where Bailey is hiding in Mary's room with Percy. Bailey dives underneath Mary's bed and Percy attempts to hide, but Clark finds them both. He shoots Percy after learning he's a surgeon but spares Bailey because she lies about her job.

Chandra Wilson That was so exciting to me, to be under that bed watching the feet go by, watching Robert getting dragged away. I just loved the terror of that and wanting the audience to have a good time with the fact that Bailey was scared to death. Mandy wasn't supposed to say anything other than cry under her sheet. We shot it from a few angles. We had a high wide one, and then we got a low shot when I got pulled from under the bed by the shooter.

Robert Baker It was pretty intense. It was a gnarly thing to shoot, but they did a good job, a faithful job of handling it, anyway. Because when I got shot, it was off-screen. You're under the bed with Bailey, you hear the shot, and then I fall. The fact that I was begging him not to shoot me wasn't seen, so I was probably a little bigger with it than I would have been if it had been a close-up or something. But that way, when I hit the ground and Bailey sees me, it was that much of an intense thing. It was very still and quiet when we weren't shooting, and it was not one of your more fun days at work.

Chandra Wilson I never got tired of it. I totally laughed, it was so hysterical.

Gary eventually finds Derek, who tells him that he should go find someplace safe so he doesn't get hurt. "I'm already hurt," replies Gary. "You hurt me when you decided to kill my wife." He then fires a bullet into Derek's chest.

Michael O'Neill Shonda's a brilliant writer. One of the things she did with that character is to allow me to try to maintain humanity even in the insanity of it. He was an incredibly broken man who felt that he hadn't protected his wife and lost it. I think she was making a statement. One is that we don't do a real good enough job in hospitals of realizing the effect of decisions on a spouse. The other is the easy availability of guns. There is a monologue at the end. I say I went to the superstore and bought a gun and ammunition that was on sale. I brought so much of it and now I have one bullet left. It's still very emotional for me. Every time there is a workplace shooting I'm rocked back on my heels.

Rob Corn Michael O' Neill, who is the nicest man ever, was spectacularly sinister. Whenever you could get extreme close-ups of his performance, it elevated the scare element.

> *Despite the best efforts of Bailey and Mary, Percy dies by the elevator. His dying wish is for Bailey to find Reed and tell her "I always had a crush on her. I don't think she knows. Tell her I loved her so much . . . tell her I was a catch. You tell her I was a hot, hot catch and she missed out on a great guy."*

Robert Baker My death was great! Like, it takes me two episodes to finally kick. I think I have been in seventy-five different shows and movies, and I have died in almost twenty of them. So I was pretty well practiced at that. That one was the best-written and the most sympathetic death that a character I'd done had had, that's for sure.

Rob Corn Standards and Practices is and was always concerned. Both episodes had opportunities for showing lots of blood, so we went for it. If my memory serves me, we even added some pooling blood digitally to make it more visual.

Tom Burman For me, little splats and blood drips are much more effective than when you do a five-gallon can and pour blood out all over the place. I hate that.

Michael O'Neill A casting woman called me [after the episode aired] and said, "Michael, it's one of the most beautiful, moving performances and horrific performances I've ever seen. But you're not going to work for a year. You can shave your head, you can shave your mustache. Nobody is going to hire you." She meant it in a benevolent way, but I had three small kids I was trying to support, so I was a little concerned. A producer asked me not long ago if I would do the same role now and I said, "No. I don't think I can do it now." I'm older. Life looks different to me now. My kids are pretty much grown and I'm not trying to keep a roof over their heads. But it was compelling television, and I'm so grateful that Shonda trusted me with it.

> "Song Beneath the Song"
> Season Seven, Episode Eighteen
> Written by Shonda Rhimes
> Directed by Tony Phelan

It's become a rite of passage for most TV shows to do a musical episode, and *Grey's Anatomy* was no exception. Inspired, in part, by how some of her writers loved musicals and a few of her stars were multi-hyphenates, Shonda Rhimes penned an episode that featured Sara Ramirez, Kevin McKidd, and Chandra Wilson singing the pop songs that were made famous on the series. Oh, and there was an actual story line, too: Callie (Ramirez) goes into cardiac arrest after she and Arizona (Jessica Capshaw) got into a car crash. The episode didn't exactly resonate with critics, but can you honestly remember any other episode from season seven? Yeah, I can't, either.

Stacy McKee We'd been talking about this notion of a musical episode for such a long time. It was always a little bit of a fantastic joke we'd never actually do, and then we did it.

Shonda Rhimes I wanted to do this ever since we started, because I'm a musical theater geek. It seemed fun, so why not try it?

Tony Phelan We took one of our soundstages, which we used as a rehearsal room, and put in couches and carpets, and we had a small band and four music stands—one each for Shonda, Sara, Kevin McKidd, and Chandra Wilson. We invited the studio and the network execs there on a Saturday morning. We had mimosas and breakfast, and then we did a presentation where the three actors sang most of the songs. Then, Shonda told the story of the musical episode. At the end of that cabaret they left, saying, "Go ahead and do it." We'd all by that point been doing the show for seven years. Part of our job as show-runners at that point was keeping people engaged and challenged. You also want to keep challenging yourself. So around that time, we did a war episode, some film noir, and a musical. We were looking for ways to stylistically play around with the show.

Sarah Drew I remember when Tony [told the cast], "Guess what? We're doing a musical episode! Who's excited?" I shot my arm into the air and nobody else did. I remember being so excited while everybody else was like, "Oh my gosh, what are we doing?" I remember calling him and being like, "I'm a singer, can't I have more to do in this episode?" He was like, "I know you're a singer. It's just because of the story we're specifically telling with the characters. There isn't a full-blown song for you to do."

Tony Phelan She was very excited and was totally game for the whole thing, and was great. We got to use her, so that was fun. But yeah, there was reluctance [among the actors]. I think getting people out of their comfort zone was a big deal. And I don't think it's any secret that the biggest resistance we had was from the studio. The studio and the network didn't think we should do it.

Sarah Drew For that big first scene where we're all singing "How to Save a Life" and surrounding Sara Ramirez on the gurney, we had a whole day of rehearsal just to get the choreography of all the medical things we were doing on which part of the song, like figuring out where the camera's going to be on which person. It was a very complicated, specific choreography, but I loved it. I ate that up. It felt like theater and made me so happy.

Shonda Rhimes There [were] no dance numbers. There [was] no singing and dancing in the halls.

Tony Phelan Ellen sang. I believe the only two people who didn't sing were Patrick and Sandra. I was really happy with it and, funny enough, we did a benefit for the Actors Fund at Royce Hall in Los Angeles where we had the cast performing the songs live. That benefit sold out in two days and we had people from around the world come see it. A whole contingent from Australia, Japan, Europe . . . super fans who loved the show and wanted to see it. I was very happy with it and I think it was one of the things as a director that I'm most proud of.

"Readiness Is All"
Season Nine, Episode Twenty-Three
Written by William Harper
Directed by Tony Phelan

In the midst of a serious episode about a pregnant Meredith tumbling down the stairs and the surgeons operating on a "human shish kebab," Matthew (Justin Bruening) surprises April with a flash bomb proposal outside of the ER. Choreographer Tyce Diorio, who was also a guest judge on *So You Think You Can Dance*, taught a bunch of extras to dance to "I Would Walk 500 Miles" from The Proclaimers while the cast stood by and watched. "Who would have thought Kepner would have found someone as dorky as she is?" quipped Karev in the scene.

Justin Bruening That was another moment of Shonda having fun with me, where I didn't know I was doing the dance number. I walked into the table read and there was a little CD player there. I'm like, "That's new. What's that for?" And she just grins and goes, "You'll find out."

Sarah Drew I knew it was coming at the beginning of the season because Tony Phelan had told me that was his plan. I was so excited about it all. I remember watching multiple YouTube videos of flash bomb proposals, just in anticipation.

Nicole Rubio I bring the patient in and it's April who goes to the ambulance and opens the door. Then the patient bolts up and we start dancing. And she's like, "What is going on?" Other people come out of the woodwork and we're all doing this dance and here comes paramedic Matthew.

Justin Bruening It was the first time the cast really got to know me and I could show them what I can do. It was nerve-racking, but I was excited for the challenge. Part of being an actor is you get thrown into situations that are extraordinary and really explore why a character is doing something and what his motivation is for doing such a grand gesture.

Sarah Drew I loved that we had all these rehearsals for it. I felt like a princess and the queen because people are, like, carrying me around, and it's all about April and these people are dancing and you just feel like you're in a musical. It made me so happy. It was so, so, so fun.

Nicole Rubio Some of the dancers were icons. The choreographer's pool of dancers included a lot of these dancers who danced with Madonna and Michael Jackson. The "Thriller" video. Just working with those professionals was such an experience. When would I ever get that experience?

Justin Bruening I think it truly was just to embarrass April, I don't know. Matthew absolutely loved April. He wanted to show that in the grandest of ways.

"The Sound of Silence"
Season Twelve, Episode Nine
Written by Stacy McKee
Directed by Denzel Washington

To spice things up in the twelfth season, Rhimes brought in Denzel Washington to direct an episode that focused on Meredith recovering after being brutally attacked by a patient.

Stacy McKee We had talked, in the writers' room, for a while, about variations on another powerful, stand-alone-type episode for Ellen. I had kind of become the go-to "sp'episode" [special episode] writer over the years—I really loved pitching them and writing them; it's so fun creatively to shake things up! The inspiration was a combination of things: an idea I'd loved for a long time, and the fact that we were going to have such an unexpected director! A few of us knew that it was possible Denzel might direct one of our episodes that season since he's friends with Debbie [Allen]. She was instrumental! But scheduling it was tricky—we weren't sure when he would actually be available, but we knew we would want a dynamic episode for him to direct. We just didn't know which one it would be. I'd pitched variations on all-silent story lines or all-silent characters/stories in the past, too, but we hadn't ever landed on the perfect way to do it.

Ellen Pompeo Debbie Allen kept teasing me weeks before, "I have a surprise for you, G!" She calls me Ghetto, so my nickname is G. I didn't know what it was going to be; I just left it alone. And then when she told me that Denzel was coming to direct, I obviously had a heart attack. I was probably a complete idiot when I met him. To be honest, directing one-hour dramas is very technical, and it's a ton of work. Most directors who come in are so overwhelmed with the technical aspects, they figure we've been doing this forever so they probably shouldn't try to tell us what to do, and a lot of them shouldn't, because they don't have great ideas anyway. Denzel was so refreshing. He's someone who wants us to know all the answers. He doesn't want you to show up to set asking a million questions. That was pretty much a whole episode of no dialogue, which was amazing and so fun. I'm as decisive and opinionated as they come, so I was fully prepared. I had to bring my A-game for him, so I did.

Stacy McKee It all came together very quickly, as soon as we got word Denzel was confirmed. I think I just walked into the writers' room that afternoon and told them to stop everything and order some dinner, because we were now putting this epi-sode together ASAP, since the directing slot Denzel was booked for was around the corner! I knew the episode needed to be powerful, and dynamic, and Meredith-centric. That's when a really phenomenal staff of writers is so important and such a blessing. That episode came together in record time—truly. It was amazing. I wasn't worried about Ellen not having lines; she can convey so much just with a glance of her eyes! I was more worried about how hard it is to be in so many scenes, back-to-back—it's such hard work. I wrote another all-Ellen ep-isode seasons before, too, where I believe she was in every sin-gle scene. I knew firsthand how much stamina that takes. But we talked through everything and she was wonderfully game. I think having Denzel there was really invigorating for every-body!

"Silent All These Years"
Season Fifteen, Episode Nineteen
Written by Elisabeth R. Finch
Directed by Debbie Allen

In this stand-alone episode that was egregiously overlooked by Emmy voters, a victim of sexual assault (played by Khalilah Joi) is treated with extraordinary kindness and support from the women of Grey Sloan Memorial.

Krista Vernoff There was a situation in our political sphere that was incredibly painful and damaging. It was Christine Blasey Ford's testimony [regarding the nomination of Brett Ka-vanaugh to the U.S. Supreme Court] and how it didn't mean anything. It hurt our souls. I went to the writers and said, "The message that has just been sent to all young women is that consent doesn't matter. We have an opportunity here to teach men and women about consent and to talk about how lasting and impactful rape can be for generations." It's the first time ever that I reached out to the staff with an actual issue as opposed to saying, "Hey! I have a character idea."

Elisabeth R. Finch (Writer) Three years [prior], the Writers Guild of America sent out an email about an opportunity for a small group of people to visit the UCLA Medical Center, Santa Monica Rape Treatment Center. It's an internationally known organization that every treatment center ought to be because of the way they have designed their space. One of the most fascinating things about this place is how every time we would go into a room, there would be a series of radio [communications] from a person who checks to see if the hallways are clear. They want to make sure no stranger, not anyone, is walking through that hallway while a survivor is passing through. I thought it was incredible that a place would design an entire program around one survivor. A year later, I watched a YouTube video of someone who donated organs. Part of the hospital protocol is that whenever an organ donor is wheeled down a hallway, every single doctor in that hospital lines the hallways to honor that person. Something clicked in my head about marrying those two things.

Krista Vernoff She pitched this scene to me as the "army of awesome," which was lining the hallways with women who would just stand there and witness this survivor's journey to protect her. It's so rare to get that kind of representation in TV that looks at the fallout of violence and focuses on ways we can support and heal each other rather than further damage each other. As a showrunner, when you hear a scene like that, you go, "Yes, please, and make it the entire episode."

Debbie Allen (Executive Producer/Dr. Catherine Avery) Honestly, I was almost paralyzed with a mix of emotions [from reading the script]. This story is so layered. It was a very emotional, personal read for me.

Krista Vernoff From the moment the script was published, there was a big reaction to it at Shondaland. Everybody was blown away. We started having people come up and ask if they could be in that scene. The women in that hallway are almost all the women on the writing staff. Many of the women are on the crew, or they are assistants at Shondaland, or they are women who work at ABC. I think there were more than a hundred women.

Elisabeth R. Finch I was the only one who went in kicking and screaming.

Krista Vernoff We forced her to do it. She is camera shy, but she had to be a part of it. She is on the screen's right side, pulling the gurney.

Elisabeth R. Finch I am not a crier. But I could barely keep myself together to walk down that hallway, over and over.

Debbie Allen We had to start dancing in the middle of shooting because it was very heavy. We didn't have all day. We had women who were leaving their jobs to come be in the scene. I had a good hour to shoot it. So we lit it and we hit it.

Krista Vernoff There was reverence in that hallway. The feeling that every woman in that room had some kind of relationship to this story was simultaneously devastating and powerfully healing. In this moment we got to say, "There are better ways we can all come together. We can witness each other. We can change."

Debbie Allen *Grey's Anatomy* is about a lot of things. We tackle the most controversial and relevant subject matters as well as wonderful relationships and people trying to find their way. And we will continue. It's part of the reason why we're like a brand-new show as we go into season sixteen. We go to the same river, but we step in new water every time.

CHAPTER 12

"Trauma Always Leaves a Scar,"
Or, The Most Heartbreaking Departures
and Deaths

When a show lasts as long as *Grey's Anatomy*, it's natural to expect that most cast members—if not all of them—will want to hit the road someday. No matter how great the salary is, playing the same role year after year can take an emotional (and sometimes physical) toll. It's the same sentiment for the writers: How many grueling surgeries and bad relationships can one character endure before you run out of story? In television, everyone has an expiration date.

If you're lucky enough—or, more specifically, if your name is Sandra Oh—you get the perfect goodbye. After giving Shonda Rhimes plenty of notice about wanting to leave at the end of season ten, Oh just had one very important request for her final episode, which she told *Entertainment Weekly* in 2014: "Please! I would like my character to remain alive."

Sandra Oh I think I had been slowly processing the decision [to leave] over the prior year and a half.

Shonda Rhimes When Cristina left, I was like, I don't know what I'm going to do. Meredith's alone. How's she going to survive? Sandra and I got together and had this really amazing conversation where I told her, "I think that my best friend for the past ten years has been a fictional character."

Mark Wilding I think what happens is, the actors think they've got the golden ticket, but at the same time, it's also golden handcuffs. Like, "I'm sort of stuck here doing this." It's a great run, but they want to go off and do something else.

Jeannine Renshaw Sandra is a very, very thoughtful actress, and very professional. She's an artist. She really wanted to have a hand in how her character that she loved and nurtured for all those years was going to leave the show. We worked with her to have the best goodbye she could possibly get.

Jenna Bans It's a huge responsibility to figure out how to give someone a great send-off that will at least, if not make the fans happy, be satisfying story-wise.

Moe Irvin Sandra Oh is a fucking freight train. I'm convinced you can put anything in front of her. That woman is something else. I remember early on with maybe the second or third episode, she had a load of dialogue at this read-through. After it was done we literally gave her a standing ovation. We were clapping for her, because she's so good.

One of the last guest actors to work with Oh was Rebecca Field, who played the mother of three children who each developed cases of cardiomyopathy.

Rebecca Field (Sabine McNeil) I think they were keeping [Oh's departure] quiet. Once I had been there a couple of times, I just asked her and said, "Oh, that's so sad but wonderful." She seemed really grateful for her time there, and sad as well. She said something like, this was her family and it was going to be really hard for her to leave, but she was also very excited to see what the future held because she had been lucky enough to be on that show for a long time. I could tell it was a very loving, warm set and people were family. I know from her point of view, it was very bittersweet.

Sandra Oh As much of my life as I feel like I [gave that] character, she has saved me and helped me grow into the artist that I am. . . . If [Shonda] didn't ask me to come back for the series finale, I would hurt her.

Shonda Rhimes I thought it was interesting that Cristina got the happiest ending of any character that I can imagine.

She wasn't kidding. Many of the show's high-profile departures were either surprisingly abrupt or shrouded in mystery and/or controversy. Case in point: After Jerrika Hinton stopped playing Dr. Stephanie Edwards in 2017, rumors persisted that her relationship with Ellen Pompeo—specifically, how Hinton liked to take personal photos on set without asking Pompeo's permission—had hastened her departure from

*the show. Hinton declined to address the situation for this
book, but her comments to EW's Natalie Abrams at the time
seemed to suggest the situation was a bit more complicated
than her just deciding to leave one day.*

Jerrika Hinton I've been there for five years, and the decision to leave was my own that was supported in a very deep way that I could never communicate, by my boss, and a host of other things that I could mention that have happened in those five years that are just significant memories.

Norman Leavitt Jerrika was always laughing, but maybe she was a little naive. She hadn't been around a lot, so maybe she didn't quite understand the power Ellen had. If she'd gone and said, "Is it okay if I take these Polaroids?" Ellen probably would've gone, "Okay." But by just doing it and not including her, you're setting yourself up for disaster.

Shonda Rhimes Actors evolve differently, and when an actor like Jerrika comes to me and says she wants to try something new creatively, I like to honor that. Jerrika has shared so much of herself with Stephanie, and I am incredibly proud of the journey we've taken together. While I'm sad to see Stephanie leave Grey Sloan Memorial, I'm excited to see what's next for Jerrika.

*As for other cast members, walking papers were issued in
myriad ways, for myriad reasons.*

Jenna Bans Sometimes it's nothing dramatic. You're just like, "Well, that's kind of all the story I have to tell for that someone."

Gaius Charles Typically you get a phone call from your reps, followed up by a phone call from producers. That was the case for me.

Tessa Ferrer This is the way the show goes. People die, they get lost in a fire, a plane accident. It's high drama. Anyone's at risk. No one's safe. Shonda and Betsy, whom I adore, were brilliant, and they were nothing but kind to me. They called and said, "We love you. We don't need your character anymore. That's it." That's just how it was.

Steven W. Bailey I never found out. I was never officially written off or anything. It just became an issue of economics, like so many things in Hollywood. They just basically determined that I was not adding any value to the show, so they didn't want to pay me. I wanted some more money and they didn't really want to pay it. But then they begrudgingly said yes. Then I went through this weird season where I kept being notified that I'm in the next episode because the writers wanted to use me and then someone with a red pen got hold of the script and I'd be called back two days later to be told, "No, you're not going to be in it because we don't want to pay you to come in." It was kind of like, "All right." I don't feel like I left. I don't feel like anybody fired me. It just sort of stopped happening. A lot of the scenes that were in the bar got replaced by the elevator. I don't know if people realized that. That was a device to save money. Some of those scenes were written for the bar first, but then you've got to pay a bunch of background performers, you've got to pay me, and there's the bar set. They said, "Wait a minute! We can have these two have a cute conversation in an elevator by themselves instead of going over to the bar."

Sarah Utterback I remember being at a table read and finding out. Literally being there, you read and you go, "Oh, this is it. This is it." And everyone's looking at you like, "This is it. This is goodbye for Olivia." It was the merger of the two hospitals, people were getting cut. There was a scene that I had with Patrick Dempsey with the most beautiful goodbye. I got to hug him, like, thirty times. Thirty takes, from every different angle. Dr. Shepherd was giving Olivia a hug goodbye, and it was really sweet and kind. There was nothing crazy, it was just a simple layoff. I got laid off. And then I was brought back, I was in this episode with my son. It was kind of revealing where Olivia is now. She's become a mom and she's moved on, and I kind of got to come back and give a little poke to Karev. Like a "hey, I was shamed but he got away with it" kind of thing. I think the writers realized that and they got to kind of correct that.

Tina Majorino Unfortunately, I was already committed to another project, so from the beginning, my time at *Grey's* was limited. I know this sounds strange, but I was really honored when I learned that Heather would die off on the show. *Grey's* is famous for very gut-wrenching, heartbreaking, emotional deaths, and having been such a fan, I felt very cool to be added to that list. They really gave Heather an amazing send-off, and I loved that they honored the character that way. I know fans were not pleased by it, but it was obviously incredibly effective, which is the goal when you're trying to make something meaningful.

Sophia Ali (Dr. Dahlia Qadri) I went off to go shoot this new Amazon pilot in New Zealand. I kind of secretly wanted a juicy death scene, but I didn't get it. I'm glad I got a chance to show Dahlia's fight a little bit. They knew I was leaving in

September, so they had a certain amount of time to write her out. They were thinking maybe there's a chance that maybe they could bring me back if they wanted to. They were leaving it open-ended.

Mark Saul Sometimes I would go a while without getting a call. It was never guaranteed that I would ever be in more episodes, and then when I would get a phone call I would always be pleasantly surprised. I have so much gratitude for them that if they didn't call me back, it's not the end of the world. The episode didn't need my character, and I feel like that's what I mostly learned from being in the writers' room. It wasn't anything personal.

Robert Baker They didn't want to kill me. They told me that. They were just like, "We just don't have anything. We just don't know what to do with your character." And at that point, I want to say there were fifteen regulars or something. It was a huge cast. Pretty much all the original cast was still there, and then they brought on the four of us. Kim Raver came on in that year. Sara Ramirez was on. It was just a huge cast. At the table read I got up and went to the bathroom after I died in the script. I guess Shonda was like, "Did you guys not tell him he was dying?" I think she thought I had to excuse myself from the room.

Lauren Stamile I wanted to stay on the show forever! But Rose had served her purpose to move the story forward. She knew that Derek and Meredith should be together and her presence was causing a problem. The best decision for her was just to exit. I think that it showed that Rose had integrity and self-awareness and I appreciated that.

Nora Zehetner I knew my character arc was wrapping up, but I didn't know I was going to die as opposed to just going off in the world to another hospital. I didn't have any control over it. If I had, I would have saved a baby or something before I died instead of sleeping with Mark Sloan.

Kim Raver had a rather abrupt exit in season eight as Dr. Teddy Altman, only to come back in season fourteen to stay indefinitely. Her first goodbye on the show was gut-wrenching because, while grieving over her dead husband, Henry (Scott Foley), she told her former lover Owen (Kevin McKidd) that she hated him.

Jeannine Renshaw It was hard to find stories for Kim [at that time]. We wanted Owen to be with Sandra Oh, so it was like, Who is he going to pick? Cristina or Teddy? It was getting harder and harder to find a place for her in the stories. No fault of hers, but once Henry died, that was such a moving, gripping story, and it just felt like we hadn't given her a lot of other things that could then foment into a story.

Kim Raver I called Shonda and said, "Isn't this a little too harsh?"She was like, "You've got to go for it." It had to come from such a place of pain that Teddy couldn't even express her grief and the only person she could do it with was her person. I was wrecked when Scott's character died, but it was so wonderfully complicated with Cristina and Owen. It was an incredible collage of complexity, which was a gift.

Brooke Smith was a huge fan favorite for her portrayal of Dr. Erica Hahn, a cardiothoracic surgeon who was dubbed "the new Burke." After sleeping with Callie for the first time in season five, Erica gave what was lovingly nicknamed the "leaves speech" for comparing their sexual experience to getting glasses as a child. "Suddenly, I yelled," she said after putting on the new specs. "The big green blobs I had been staring at my whole life, they weren't big green blobs. They were leaves, on trees. And I didn't even know I was missing leaves! I didn't even know leaves existed! And then: leaves!" Erica gazes at Callie with teary eyes and declares, "You are glasses. I am so gay." Shortly after shooting that episode, the decision was made to yank Smith off the show. Smith didn't see it coming.

Brooke Smith I know Shonda was very happy with the leaves scene. The next thing I heard was a message from the assistant director saying she wanted to see me after I wrapped. I had my Prius key in my hand the whole time. I guess I remember that I was squeezing it. I was totally blindsided. When she told me that I was going to be let go or fired or whatever, I said, "When?" And she was like, "This is your last episode." We were already shooting it. I was like, "What's going to happen to me?" I know there was quite a bit of time between when I was told and when the episode aired. I was asked to make a statement. Like, right when they told me, they said, "Maybe we should make a statement." Why would we do that? I said, "Let's let the episode play and then when I'm gone, we'll just make a statement then." It definitely felt like the order came from above. It was clear Steve didn't like me. I mean, I do remember him coming to visit the set about two weeks before I got fired. I remember asking, "Who is that guy?" Someone replied, "What do you mean who is that guy? That's the head of ABC!" Well, surely, I was thinking to myself, he's going to introduce himself, right? He never did.

Mark Wilding Steve McPherson made his decision and then that was that. She was gone. It was one of those things where we were told he didn't like her, so get rid of her. Then we came up with a six-episode arc to ease her out of the show. But it was like, "No, you don't understand. Get rid of her *now.*" We had to do it in the here and now.

Stephen McPherson I don't even remember who [Brooke Smith] was. This is why I left and hate the entertainment biz. I pity people like her—delusional blame and hate directed toward others in attempts to make themselves feel better. I had nothing to do with anything regarding her, including even casting her. When you're in a position like I was, there is a daily onslaught of hate pointed at you, as people want to blame their own failures on someone.

Tony Phelan All I know is that Shonda came into the room and said we were going to go in a different direction with that character. She wanted to write her off in the best way that we could and so we did. I don't know who was the genesis of that decision.

Brooke Smith I loved Hahn. I thought she was great. I feel bad that she didn't have a proper send-off. I remember at the time, like, "Oh my God, what a coup. How did I get here?"

Because I was never a popular kid in high school and this was like the popular show, you know? I felt like all of a sudden they made me a cheerleader or something. Every day I just couldn't believe it. I'm still hurt by Shonda, because I never heard from her again after that day. I guess part of me thought maybe, just maybe, she just didn't like the character and fired me. I have no idea. But if it was some order from above or whatever, I just kind of hoped that she would fight for her characters a little more.

Shonda Rhimes Sara Ramirez [was] an incredible comedic and dramatic actress and we wanted to be able to play up her magic. Unfortunately, we did not find that the magic and chemistry with Brooke's character would sustain in the long run.

Mark Wilding It's very funny, because as a writer you get grief when someone didn't get a very good send-off. Sometimes there are orders from on high and you have no choice. Even if you're Shonda Rhimes, you don't have a choice.

Jenna Bans We all really liked Brooke. And she's a great actor.

Brooke Smith I'm nervous around suits to this day. Like, *really* nervous. When I was in school they told us table reads were for the actors to start exploring the characters. It wasn't supposed to be like a full-blown performance, ready to shoot. Because now it is. You hear about actors getting fired right after a table read all the time now.

Bidding farewell to Eric Dane, aka McSteamy, was also particularly tough for the writers. Though he was a highly

*respected plastic surgeon, Mark Sloan's best attributes were
how he brought levity—and a great set of abs—to the halls
of Seattle Grace.*

Shonda Rhimes When Mark Sloan first appeared on *Grey's
Anatomy* in season two, the original idea was to have him do
one episode. But none of us planned on what would happen
once we cast Eric Dane. His Mark Sloan wasn't just flirty and
handsome—Eric's Mark Sloan was dirty and hot but also completely self-aware of what he was lacking in emotion and self-
control. Eric's Mark Sloan was smart enough to know he was a
man-whore and sexy enough to make the audience believe in
him anyway.

Eric Dane Dr Sloan's the most flawed. He [was] just trying
to cope with his issues . . . and using some pretty interesting
tools to cope.

Mimi Melgaard That towel scene was just priceless. When
he comes out of the bathroom to Addison, just ripped and with
only a towel on. It was like, "Whew!" That towel was still hanging in the storeroom before I left. It should go in the Smithso-
nian: "This is the Eric Dane towel!"

Shonda Rhimes One of my favorite moments ever.

Mark Wilding I always liked writing for the Mark Sloan
character, just because he was a little more crass. But he was
charming, too.

Shonda Rhimes He seduces so many nurses that they form
an actual organization dedicated to eradicating him: Nurses
United Against Mark Sloan!

Sarah Utterback I think there was a line that I had about him being kind of grabby in the workplace. Olivia was not a fan of being groped in the workplace. I mean, isn't that amazing? This was all pre-#MeToo.

Shonda Rhimes But he also [helped] a lonely man change his gender. He rebuilds the face of Jane Doe. He fixes cleft palates and lionitis bone deformities and builds a little boy a pair of ears. He performs double arm transplants. He helps Callie recognize that her feelings for another woman are not something to be ignored. Okay, yes, he sleeps with his best friend's wife. But he also supports his daughter when she chooses to put her baby up for adoption. Yes, he breaks his penis having sex with Lexie Grey. But he also falls madly in love with her. He's a good man, Mark Sloan. Well, he was a good man.

Dane and Chyler Leigh sizzled, despite a difference in their ages. But their love was not meant to be: Lexie died in the plane crash at the end of season eight because Leigh wanted off the show to pursue other projects, while Mark succumbed to his injuries from the same disaster the following year. In a statement at the time, Shonda Rhimes made it sound like a decision that she and Dane made together, if not Dane's alone: "It felt like the right time for him. I love Eric, and Eric and I have been working together for a long time, so it was bittersweet. I'm happy he's going to go on and do other things." But economics may have had a lot more to do with it.

Jeannine Renshaw Everyone wanted to keep McSteamy alive. He was a wonderful character to write for, very funny.

I don't think anybody wanted him to die. As I recall, it was a budget thing. We had to get rid of somebody. So I don't think anybody wanted to kill anybody. Chyler had asked to leave, so then we just felt like . . . yeah, it was time, story-wise. You have to lose people on that show.

Mark Wilding We were surprised by the chemistry between Mark Sloan and Lexie early on. We were like, "Wow, they should be a couple." That was just interesting for us.

Shonda Rhimes I like to believe that Mark is with Lexie somewhere. That those two characters are spending eternity together, getting to have the relationship they were never able to have when they were alive.

If only George O'Malley had someone waiting for him on the other side. By the time the decision was made to kill off T. R. Knight's character in the season five finale, it ended a long and supposedly uncomfortable period between him and Rhimes. The tension seemed to start after he followed the Isaiah Washington incident by announcing he was gay.

T. R. Knight I think she was concerned about having my statement come out so close to the [initial] event.

Shonda Rhimes I said, "If you want to come out, that's awesome. We'll totally support you." And then he went away, thought about it, and came back and said, "I'm going to make this statement." I remember saying to Betsy Beers, "This is our proudest day here. T.R. got to come out, and I got to say to him that it wouldn't affect his character," because he was concerned that he was going to come out and George would suddenly be gay. I was like, "We aren't going to do that." The idea that a gay actor can't play a straight man is insulting.

But then Knight saw his screen time diminish in seasons four and five, so when it came time to discuss his charac- ter's future with Rhimes, Knight said he would rather leave instead.

T. R. Knight There just comes a time when it's so clear that moving on is the best decision.

Shonda Rhimes I wasn't done telling stories for him. We used to joke that George would be the last person wheeled out of the hospital as chief of surgery. I looked in his face and he was really sure.

Katherine Heigl I didn't think it was the right decision. I felt like some of the problems could be worked through or looked at differently or tolerated, because it [was] a good job on so many levels.

Mark Wilding I just think he wanted to go do something else, frankly. I don't know that he was happy on the show at that point. I don't really think it was a breakdown in commu- nication so much as it was he just didn't want to do the show anymore.

T. R. Knight My five-year experience proved to me that I could not trust any answer that was given [about George]. . . . I never made any demands, like, "You do this, or else." I was always very respectful. In any sort of creative process, there are going to be disagreements.

*The decision to literally throw George under a bus after sav-
ing a stranger was not an easy one for the writers.*

Mark Wilding He was our first major character to actually
get killed off. You're always faced with the dilemma of having
him go to another hospital or dying in a heroic manner. Here's
the thing about the show: we wanted to go for hard laughs, but
we also wanted to go for really emotional moments, for people
to get really caught up in and moved.

Jeannine Renshaw You have to lose people on that show.
That's what's so great about Shonda. Shonda was willing to
lose people and to have people die, which felt sort of new and
fresh. And then *Game of Thrones* started doing it and everyone
was talking about how *Game of Thrones* was so willing to kill
people. I was like, "Shonda's been doing that forever on *Grey's
Anatomy.*"

Jenna Bans That was really hard to figure out what to do.
You realize as a writer that so many people love and live with
the characters; that it's kind of a huge responsibility to figure
out how to give them a great send-off that will at least, if not
make the fans happy, be satisfying story-wise. George leaves to
join the military toward the end of that season and he gets in
a horrible accident. Meredith is taking care of this disfigured,
injured patient. And at the very end, he writes what they all call
him from season one, 007, on her palm with his finger. That's
the moment she realizes it's him. I think when Shonda pitched
that, we all got chills in the room.

Mark Saul I just remember my jaw dropping when I read
that the first time. It was so clever and heartbreaking. It came

out of nowhere for me, so I was really impressed with the writers' ability to do that.

In fact, Knight didn't have to show up for those final episodes. Any extra could have worn the disfiguring prosthetic on his face. But Knight was determined to work until the very end.

Mark Wilding He wanted to really throw himself into it all the way. He wanted to do his own fight scenes, even when we had a scene where he and Alex fight in that episode where we went up to Seattle. He didn't want to wear pads or anything. He was very much like, "I'm gonna play this all the way." More power to him.

Norman Leavitt It was just weird, the whole thing. It was really uncomfortable and T.R. didn't need to be there. He chose to do it. He was real Method.

Tom Burman He wanted off the show, so they literally threw him under the bus. He never complained once, and when we had his whole head covered, he never complained once. They punished him for wanting to get off the show. Petty, huh?

Jenna Bans Although it was completely tragic, he died in service to other people. We felt like that was a really important part of his character. And not only was he leaving to join the military, he got hit by a bus because he was pushing someone else out of the way. We felt like he definitely died a hero. That was something collectively as the writers' room we wanted to give that character.

Nicole Rubio It was so sad for many reasons. Obviously it was something he felt compelled to do. When someone is moving on to try different things, you wish them well. But man, I loved that George. I loved working with T.R. It's like you start losing the foundation. The foundation starts to shift a bit. And then can you hold that foundation together with the rest of the bricks that you have?

T. R. Knight There were so many wonderful experiences. [After] doing so much theater, to be able to spend five years with some really remarkable people, and also get to constantly explore acting in front of a camera for that time, there's so much I learned from [*Grey's*] as a person, and also just as an actor, that it informs everything, but in a way that I'm really grateful that it informs everything. It leaves me with a very grateful and thankful heart.

> *Rhimes tried to convince Knight to return in flashbacks for the first episodes of season six, but to no avail. Still, fans did get one last look at their beloved George, and it was breathtaking: he's quietly standing in uniform while looking at Izzie standing in the elevator, wearing her pink prom dress.*

T. R. Knight To me it was so powerful. I thought it was the best way to leave it.

> *Ten years is a long time to be on a show—just ask Sandra Oh—so it wasn't too much of a surprise that Sara Ramirez was ready to throw in the towel at the end of season twelve. But the way that she did it was very unexpected, both for fans and for Shonda Rhimes. First, the actress tweeted, "That's a*

wrap for Doctor #CallieTorres @Season 13 #Grey's Anatomy. Thank you all for an enriching & unforgettable #rollercoaster ride!" Then she released a statement saying, "I'm deeply grateful to have spent the last 10 years with my family at Grey's Anatomy and ABC, but for now I'm taking some welcome time off. Shonda's been so incredible to work for, and we will definitely continue our conversations! I send my love to Ellen, the rest of the cast and crew, and I look forward to always being part of the Shondaland family." Later, Rhimes revealed at the Vulture Festival in New York that she'd learned of Ramirez's decision to depart only three days before the actress made her decision public. "This one was different because it wasn't a big, planned thing," she said. "I had a different plan going, and when Sara came in and said, 'I really need to take a break,' I was lucky that we'd shot the end of the season with her going to New York."

Ramirez was a groundbreaker in so many ways—starting with how Rhimes wrote Callie specifically for her. When Oprah Winfrey came to set in 2006 to interview the cast, she asked Ramirez how she first joined the show, which is when Ramirez revealed that "it was unbelievable. I was in New York on Broadway doing a show, Spamalot, and ABC/Touchstone came to see the show. They said, 'Be on our network. Pick a show.' They sent me every show they had and Grey's Anatomy was my favorite. I was a huge fan. So they flew Shonda Rhimes out, we had breakfast, and she said, 'I'm going to write you this role. You're going to be

an orthopedic surgeon and you're going to be with George.'"
Ramirez was an immediate standout because many fans saw
themselves in her.

Sara Ramirez She's a tall, full-bodied Latina, who [was] being portrayed not as a victim of her tallness or her size. Shonda
Rhimes [wanted] to make Callie sexy. Latinas, we're in touch
with our sexuality.

Rhimes never wanted her actresses, including Ramirez, to
feel uncomfortable during sex scenes. If they didn't want to
show a lot of skin, it was always their choice to remain hid-
den under the covers. But Rhimes also wouldn't let Ramirez
sabotage her own intimate scenes by wallowing in self-doubt.

Sara Ramirez I was pretty much naked that season [when
Callie dated George]. They put me in my underwear, for God's
sake. I felt intimidated and fat. I said to [Shonda Rhimes], "Girl,
there is so much cottage cheese up in this set." She smiled and
said, "Work it." She would not entertain my insecurities. It's a
beautiful thing.

Mimi Melgaard I think everyone has moments of insecu-
rity. It doesn't matter if you're famous or not famous. You still
go, "Argh!" I was there to make sure that they looked good, and
they did look good, trust me. We all had a really great working
relationship.

Still, there were differences of opinion over whether the show
was oversexualizing Callie. Though naturally beautiful,

Ramirez still wore more makeup than the other actresses—
something that was not lost on the network or Rhimes.

Norman Leavitt We'd get notes that her hair was too much or too little or too . . . *something.* Her bright cheeks or her lips were weird. Sara was a great gal, just really wonderful, but I think she was insecure. Some of the other actresses are really attractive and have big egos. Actresses are funny, because without doing a lot, they can make another actress feel really insecure.

Jaicy Elliot (Dr. Taryn Helm) I think it is important to talk about it, because everyone's so beautiful in the cast and everyone is so slender. Everyone is just so incredibly flawless. Growing up, I definitely would have felt empowered by seeing a plus-size character on such an iconic show. I get a lot of feedback from people feeling represented. I think that that's really important, because we're in the time when images are changing and people are opening up to different realities. In real life, I'm a healthy person and I work out and eat healthy, but it's important for people to know that opportunities aren't restricted to people who are a certain type or fit in a certain box.

Callie, like Cristina, got a happy ending: she reconciled with
Arizona and reunited with Penelope in New York.

Tony Phelan I'm particularly proud that we put a relationship between a lesbian woman and a bisexual woman in America's living room. We had these two characters fall in love, get married, have children, and break up. And I think it was the relationship that a lot of people were deeply invested in, and I think it went a long way to making that kind of a relationship something that people in Middle America would now understand.

Jessica Capshaw The first season I was on, season five, when Callie and Arizona began their courtship, everything was super light and fun and sexy and exciting. There was this moment where they just danced. I don't think there was any dialogue. We went to the apartment that Callie was living in and we just danced. We had so much fun doing it. It was my favorite because it held so much promise. It was the beginning of the relationship that was just so exciting and you [didn't] know where it was going to go. It was just really lovely.

But even Ramirez seemed to indicate there was more story left in her alter ego. After Rhimes revealed that she'd tried to get Ramirez to return for Jessica Capshaw's send-off in season fourteen but was stymied by CBS, Ramirez's new network for Madam Secretary, *the actress took the time to post this 2018 tweet: "For the record @CBS has been nothing but gracious and generous to me. They are open to Callie coming back! The ball is in @ABCNetwork's court." She added the hand/peace sign and some purple heart emojis.*

Sara Ramirez Shonda and I agreed to keep the conversations going, and she knows I'm open to keeping those conversations going.

Lesley Goldberg Sara's exit came as a big surprise. Many industry observers, myself included, thought a cryptic tweet that she posted in April 2016 was an attempt to leverage her sizable and vocal fan base to bolster ongoing contract negotiations. A month later, she was gone, and the chapter on one of television's most important examples of LGBTQ+ visibility would be closed. Callie and Arizona were TV's first prime-time lesbian wedding, and the scene also happened to be my first-ever set visit to *Grey's Anatomy*. Being on location for that historic scene remains among the highlights of my career. As for Ramirez, she'd debut on CBS's *Madam Secretary* a year and a half later, and with a new look that restored the pulses of Calzona fans everywhere.

Shonda Rhimes She will always have a home at Shondaland.

If Ramirez's departure stung fans, then the news about Jessica Capshaw and Sarah Drew exiting in 2018 just about killed them. The timing was not ideal: Ellen Pompeo had just signed a $20 million–plus two-year deal that would keep her on the show through the sixteenth season. And thus a narrative emerged that Drew and Capshaw were dropped because "no producer likes to add more to the budget," one studio executive opined. Insiders insisted that one had nothing to do with the other.

Krista Vernoff As writers, our job is to follow the stories where they want to go and sometimes that means saying goodbye to characters we love.

Sarah Drew The answer that was given was, "We've put you through so much and I don't know what else to put you through," and it's a "creative decision, it's not a budgetary one." I feel like I'll never really know why. It is what it is. It's just that for someone who'd been on the show for nine years, it felt strange. We just didn't have too many people who hadn't asked to leave to be written off after such a long tenure on the show. So it felt new and different and I was confused. I must have said "I'm so confused" like ten times in that meeting. Life goes on. It happens all the time; beloved characters get written off shows all the time and it's not their fault and it's not because they've done anything wrong. When you're in the writers' room, you're trying to come up with what's going to shake things up and what's going to make things fresh and new and interesting.

Shonda Rhimes I will be forever grateful to both Jessica and Sarah for bringing these characters to life with such vibrant performances and for inspiring women around the globe. They will always be a part of our Shondaland family.

Jessica Capshaw I am grateful that I have gotten to bring [Arizona] to life and for the life that she has brought to me. I am sad to see her go, but I am consoled by the idea that she will continue to live on and on in all of our consciences and our imaginations. Shonda, thank you for the ride on this incredible roller coaster.

Sarah Drew Honestly, to speculate is, for me, a waste of time. It doesn't help me in any way to try to understand. In the aftermath I've had so many people come up to me to say, "I'm so glad you're at least alive, like, I'm so glad that April didn't die." For the sake of the fans, then, yeah, I'm glad. She had a happy ending. She discovered her new calling and she got married and that made her really happy and feel really fulfilled. I think that felt good for a lot of the fans.

And it felt good for Drew, too.

Sarah Drew There were so many beautiful things that happened because of how it went down. I wouldn't have experienced the kind of love that was thrown my way if I had just left when the show ended. I wouldn't have gotten letters from my cast mates and members of the crew. I wouldn't have had fans hire a plane to fly over the set saying, "We love Sarah Drew and Jessica Capshaw." It meant so much to me. So it's interesting how the things in life that feel really challenging can actually wind up being beautiful. I'm constantly being reminded of that in my life.

An actor who has appeared on a show since the very beginning should, at the very least, get his own sky sign. But there was no time to throw any sort of goodbye party for Justin Chambers, who released the shocking announcement in January 2020 that he was leaving the drama that made him a household name. There wasn't even a last chance to see him in scrubs, since his final episode had aired almost two months prior.

Justin Chambers There's no good time to say goodbye to a show and character that's defined so much of my life for the past fifteen years. For some time now, however, I have hoped to diversify my acting roles and career choices. And, as I turn fifty and am blessed with my remarkable, supportive wife and five wonderful children, now is that time. As I move on from *Grey's Anatomy*, I want to thank the ABC family, Shonda Rhimes, original cast members Ellen Pompeo, Chandra Wilson, and James Pickens, and the rest of the amazing cast and crew, both past and present. And, of course, the fans, for an extraordinary ride.

In an episode that aired two months later, it was revealed through a handful of letters that were sent to Meredith that Karev left Seattle to reunite with Izzie and their twins.

Krista Vernoff It's nearly impossible to say goodbye to Alex Karev. That is as true for me and for all of the writers at *Grey's Anatomy* as it is for the fans. We have loved writing Alex. And we have loved watching Justin Chambers's nuanced portrayal of him. For sixteen seasons, sixteen years, we have grown up alongside Alex Karev. We have been frustrated by his limitations and we have been inspired by his growth and we have come to love him deeply and to think of him as one of our very best friends. We will miss him terribly.

Sharon Lawrence (Robbie Stevens) I'd like to think that Robbie is in their lives. Would they let her near the grandchildren? Of course they would! Because she'd be the fun grandma. It's not like she's irresponsible. She's just emotionally kind of limited, her horizons are limited. That's all.

Jenna Bans Karev and Izzie ran the gamut. They had this ongoing push-me-pull-me romance that we had fun playing with. I saw the episode where he ended up with Izzie. Viewers loved them together.

Justin Chambers You're in a bubble [on the show]. You

wear scrubs every day, you see pretty much the same people every day, in the same four walls, the same studios, you drive the same route to work. For me it [was] sort of a factory job for acting. You just clock in, clock out. Yeah, I guess it is sentimental, but it's sort of like, "Wow, I just can't believe how fast it's gone."

Curiously, Pompeo kept her goodbye note on Instagram focused on Karev, not Chambers. "Thanks to our national treasure @ therealdebbieallen and the writers for giving Alex Karev the best send off. Thanks to @shondarhimes for creating the most amazing character. For me personally for Karev to go back to the beginning . . . was the best possible storyline. It pays homage to those incredible first years and the incredible cast . . . that created a foundation so strong that the show is still standing."

Tony Phelan I'm actually amazed that any of the originals are still there, because it's such a grind. We [he and his wife, Joan Rater] reached a point where we were like, "We have nothing more to say with these characters."

Joan Rater We wanted to leave when Sandra left. She's a good friend of ours. I just don't know. I just think it [was] probably a sad time around there.

Tony Phelan [Chambers and his wife have] been together forever.

Joan Rater The guy is truly a . . .

Tony Phelan A mensch. Five kids. Just a mensch.

Joan Rater I know there's been some nutty people on that show, which is why they're so great. But he's just normal. A normal dude.

Norman Leavitt Justin is really a wonderful guy. He has a great heart.

More than a year later, fans were caught off guard by the news that Giacomo Gianniotti's run as Dr. Andrew DeLuca had come to an end. His character was fatally stabbed in the March 11, 2021, episode—and boy did he bleed out in those final hospital scenes.

Giacomo Gianniotti I don't think people were really told before, so it was sort of a surprise to everyone. We were all on Zoom, of course, and everyone was just kind of looking up with tears in their eyes and shocked and jaws on the floor and being like, "Are you kidding me?" Because as we find out, we don't know what happens until the very end. At that time in the script, to protect the integrity of the story line, it didn't say whether he died or not. So everyone was on the edge of their seats, wanting the answer. I think my last stuff, if I'm remembering correctly, was my stuff in the OR. Strangely enough, DeLuca's end was my end, too. It was emotional. I felt like, here I am on this table, I've got blood everywhere and bleeding out, and it just made it very real.

Sarah Drew It's always sad to lose a family member because we spend so much time together. Fans might get angry and turn off the TV and stage a riot for a minute. But they'll come back. They always did.

Did Drew have a previous career as a fortune-teller or something? More than a year after she talked to me for this book, it was announced that she would be reprising her role as April for a spring of 2021 episode.

I want to change the world, instead I sleep.
I want to believe in more than you and me.
But all that I know is I'm breathing.
All I can do is keep breathing.
All we can do is keep breathing
Now . . .

—"KEEP BREATHING," INGRID MICHAELSON

No artist has contributed more to the sound and feel of *Grey's Anatomy* than Ingrid Michaelson, a New York City–born singer-songwriter who began her indie pop career in 2005 by self-releasing her studio albums *Slow the Rain* and *Girls and Boys*. After she was discovered by *Grey's* music supervisor Alexandra Patsavas, Michaelson licensed fifteen songs (and counting!) to the drama between seasons three and sixteen.

Ingrid Michaelson My first song for *Grey's Anatomy* was called "Breakable," from my album *Girls and Boys*. When I first started writing music, I was sort of a late bloomer. I was in musical theater and that's what I thought I was going to do, and I started writing after college and I really enjoyed it, so I turned my direction that way and it just worked out. I mean, I worked really hard, but it worked out. I remember, in the beginning of my career when I was writing, my mom said to me, "You know, I love *Grey's Anatomy* and the music is amazing." So she'd be like, "You should write a song for *Grey's Anatomy*." I was like, "Okay, yeah. I should also run for president." It seemed very unattainable, but I thought in my head, If my mom thinks I should do this, I should do this. I put that energy out into the world.

When my manager and I first started working together, she said, "We have a really great relationship with Alex Patsavas of Chop Shop Music Supervision." I was like, "What? *Grey's Anatomy*?" Within a couple of months of signing with Secret Road for my licensing, we got "Breakable" on the show. There was no negativity in terms of licensing my music. I very quickly came to the realization that I'm going to make money and I'm going to be able to further my career [with it]. I'm going to be able to make more music. I was working as a coffee barista and I was living at home. I had no savings.

The reason why I wrote "Keep Breathing" was because I wanted it to be in the season [three] finale of *Grey's Anatomy*. I knew they wanted original music, because they wanted to release a soundtrack. But it's not like they said, "We want you to write a song for the finale, here are some details about the show. Spoiler alert: Meredith is ripping off Sandra Oh's dress because they didn't get married." But I knew the vibe of the show and I knew what would fit.

I used to write everywhere. I'd write in bathrooms on tour, I'd write at sound check, I'd write in the green room. Everything would pour out of my heart and soul. When I finished it and sent it in to them, they were like, "We love it! We're going to use it in the finale. It's not the last song, but we're still going to use it in the third act somewhere." And I was like, "Okay, that's still pretty cool." Then a few weeks go by and they said, "You know, we've done some rethinking and reediting and we're actually going to use it for the last six minutes of season three." It was like I manifested it!

I know where I was when I watched the episode. I was in my apartment in Brooklyn and we had some people over. I remember my friend made guacamole and she kept the pit of the avocado in the guacamole to keep it from going brown. So I associate the season three finale of *Grey's* with learning how to keep guacamole from going brown. Isn't that crazy? It was such a gigantic moment because the song didn't exist anywhere yet. It wasn't on an album. "Breakable" and "The Way I Am" were on *Girls and Boys*, which was already out. But "Keep Breathing" wasn't available, so people were like, "I want this music right now." It was definitely the biggest showcase of my music.

I remember I performed at a place in New York that's not there anymore called the Living Room. Everybody played there. If packed, it held like one hundred and fifty people. When I would play, there would be like forty. My mom would come and bring her friends, so that bulked up the audience. Two or three weeks after "Breakable" aired on *Grey's Anatomy*, I was there to perform. I was going to set up my gear and meet my band and there was a line of people from the doorway. It was jam-packed. So I asked a girl at the front of the line, "Who are you here to see?" And she said, "Ingrid Michaelson." She didn't know what I looked like. But she had Googled the lyrics to the song and had downloaded "Breakable." We sold out the show, and it was because of *Grey's Anatomy*. So, to me, even though "Keep Breathing" was so gigantic and so massive, for me it was that first show after "Breakable" aired that was really telling, because the show really moved the needle for me in terms of music lovers. People who love music watch the show and they seek out the artists, and then they go see them. It's pretty incredible.

In my future recordings, I would have excess songs that wouldn't make my record, so we would always give them to Chop Shop before we pushed [them] to anybody else. And nine out of ten times they would pick [them] up and use [them] on *Grey's Anatomy*. "Turn to Stone" is one of those. It wasn't anywhere until it was on *Grey's Anatomy*. I remember writing that during a sound check. I think I was listening to a lot of Coldplay, which inspired it in terms of the melodic structure. There's no real way to decode my music. It's pretty simple what everything means. I imagine I was just feeling pretty useless and pretty stuck in whatever moment I was in when I wrote that. I remember how it was used [for Izzie and Alex's wedding], and then it was used in Justin Chambers's last episode. Chris Carmack [Dr. Atticus Lincoln] and his wife, Erin Slaver, covered it. That was really cool. I love that they brought it back.

Alex Patsavas and Chop Shop are one hundred percent the reason why I am where I am now. They gave me what radio didn't—a platform. It all comes back to that night at the Living Room. The night before, I had twenty people. After *Grey's Anatomy*, there were a hundred and fifty in the audience. It's funny, because when I watch the show I have this idea that, maybe, I could be friends with these people. We're intertwined because my music is playing behind these iconic scenes. In reality, we don't even know each other. There is a strangeness to that. But I think that's the power of music. If it's the right song and the right moment, it just clicks. Everybody is somehow magically in sync.

CHAPTER 13

"We Have to Keep Reinventing Ourselves, Almost Every Minute, Because the World Can Change in an Instant," Or, How Shonda Rhimes and Ellen Pompeo Became the Highest-Paid Women in Television

They may have developed into one of Hollywood's most dynamic duos, but Shonda Rhimes and Ellen Pompeo didn't start out as kindred spirits. In fact, their journey to Hollywood couldn't have been more disparate: Rhimes was a Yale-educated daughter of professionals who grew up outside of Chicago, while Pompeo never made it past high school, having been raised by her father in a blue-collar Boston suburb after her mother died when she was four. "I grew up around wiseguys," Pompeo told Dax Shepard's *Armchair Expert* podcast in August 2020. "I'm really like Ray Liotta in *Goodfellas*. I grew up enamored with these wiseguys who seem to have all this money and power. They drove nice cars. They wore beautiful suits. They

had beautiful girlfriends who wore fur coats. I grew up enamored with the power that money gave them. What I probably
didn't realize is they probably killed people, too, which gave
them a lot of power. I wasn't really cognizant of that fact." By
the time their two worlds collided, Rhimes was confident and
ambitious, while Pompeo was a self-described "rough around
the edges" actress who didn't seem too comfortable with head-
lining her own show. In fact, Pompeo began her run on *Grey's
Anatomy* with a very specific strategy: keep the attention focused
on the series and away from her. The actress even borrowed a
little trick from Madonna to help achieve her refreshing goal:
she'd wear the same black tracksuit to work every day to dis-
courage paparazzi from documenting her every move. Besides
keeping her out of the limelight, it was also a way to protect
Meredith.

Ellen Pompeo If they know you're going to step out with a
beautiful new bag, a beautiful dress, and beautiful new shoes,
they're going to show up like clockwork every day. But they
can't sell that same picture of you in that same outfit every day.
It's like if you know so much about Ellen Pompeo, how do you
buy me as Meredith Grey? The more you can identify with me,
the less I am Meredith Grey to you.

*Her tactics worked: for the most part, Pompeo wasn't attract-
ing a lot of attention in the show's heady years. Sandra Oh
and Patrick Dempsey earned most of the good headlines (she
snagged six Emmy nominations, while he was TV's biggest
heartthrob), while Katherine Heigl and Isaiah Washington*

got stuck with the bad ones. Pompeo, in contrast, seemed to quietly blend into the background.

Norman Leavitt In the beginning, Sandra Oh was intimidating and Patrick ran the whole deal. People would come to the set and want to see Patrick. No one wanted to see Ellen. She was kind of shuffled to the background. It was weird. Patrick was the big showman and everybody would want to see Patrick. He'd have his arms around them for photos and smiling. Ellen never sat on the set in the director chair. She would always sit away.

Jennifer Armstrong I feel like Ellen was super reserved at the beginning. She was just, like, a standard TV star . . . which is understandable. I'm sure she was guarding that job. Patrick was very much playing the McDreamy thing up. He was charming and actually learned my name and knew who I was at some point, which shouldn't be that big of a deal, but it kind of is with stars like this. They meet a lot of reporters, so it's always a little bit of a thrill when they learn to know who you are.

Despite her best efforts in those early years, Pompeo made headlines—and not the good kind. Viewers would occasionally express concern about her slight frame and her character's poor choices (like those painful one-nighters). Pompeo told Los Angeles Confidential *magazine in 2007 that "I just worry about the girls who look up to me. I don't want them to think I starve myself or don't eat, and that to be like me, that's what they have to do."*

Ellen Pompeo Success is a tricky thing. I feel like it's very easy to get caught up. I kind of have a rule, which is I don't listen to the good, so I don't have to listen to the bad. If you listen to it and you pay attention to it and you think that means something, then you're also going to think that the bad means something.

Nicholas Fonseca (Former *EW* Senior Editor) I can remember being warned more than once by the publicist who stayed with me throughout my days of visits [to the set] that questions to Ellen Pompeo around her weight were off-limits. [My editor] had wanted her to address accusations that she was too thin, and it was pretty clear the network knew we were after those quotes. I never got to ask them, though I can say Ellen was perfectly lovely in conversation and didn't seem too bothered by having to talk to a journo.

Shonda Rhimes If Meredith Grey were a man, you'd say he's interesting and brave and struggling against his own demons. A lot of women on TV are written as men would like them to be. Meredith is written like people I know.

Ellen Pompeo There's not much I can do. I've got to be okay with whatever it is I have to do and find a way to make it real for the audience, to make the audience believe it. That's my only job. I guess even if they hate my character, if they're believing my performance that's all I really care about. That's all I can control. Otherwise I'd go crazy.

Though her character's name may have been in the title, Pompeo wasn't much of a leader on set in those early days. No one was, really.

Longtime Crew Member Ellen didn't really learn her dialogue, and it drove people nuts. She and Patrick didn't particularly get along because she never memorized her dialogue.

Jeannine Renshaw That was part of the problem. It was like one big playground, and everyone was on their own. You might be on the swings with Cristina and somebody else was on the jungle gym, but it wasn't like a team playing a game. Do you know what I'm saying?

Nicole Rubio Ellen had never done her own show. I think some people are just natural-born leaders, while some people don't know that "Wow, I'm number one on the call sheet. I need to be having barbecues, or I need to be taking more of a leadership role." She was trying to stay focused on being Meredith. Her days were demanding. She was in almost every scene. So for her to be a leader, too, would take a lot of energy, a lot of time.

Norman Leavitt In the beginning, Shonda was on the set. She was there every day. She would do interviews. The first few years, she was there every moment. As the show went along and she got other shows, those became her headquarters. Those years [when Rhimes was not on set] were really hard for Ellen.

Jeannine Renshaw I think the young stars were not prepared for the longevity of the show. I think it didn't start out with an adult at the top. For example, I worked with Mark Harmon when I was Cybill Shepherd's stand-in on *Moonlighting*. I would read off-camera lines with Bruce Willis because she wouldn't stay for Bruce's coverage. Mark Harmon [who joined the show in season three as Shepherd's love interest] was just a very special kind of actor. You could tell he didn't have that

same kind of ego I was seeing in Cybill and Bruce Willis. I remember hearing that he was the leader on that set. He was an
adult. He knew how a set should run. There wasn't that on
Grey's Anatomy. There were just a bunch of young kids. James
Pickens, Jr., he wasn't in it as much at first. None of the leads
knew to take control.

Ellen Pompeo I'd much rather it [had been] steady than a
huge hit. It's not that I'm mad it was a huge hit, I'm just saying
when there's that kind of pressure a lot of people do pay attention to that, they get freaked out by it and they get affected. I
always think slow and steady wins the race every time.

*In other words, good things come to those who wait. When
the decision was made to kill off Derek, the power finally—
and deservedly—shifted to Pompeo, even when there were
doubts that Meredith, and the series, could survive without
McDreamy. After all, Derek was not "the sun," as Cristina
so memorably told her.*

Shonda Rhimes When Cristina said that, Meredith realized
that she had been taking a back seat to allow this man to get
what he wanted. In an effort not to become her mother, she had
tried too hard to become something less. What I loved about
season eleven was her saying, "That's not who I am." It was so
interesting for me to discover that audiences, especially women,
are so conditioned to believe that there's a singular fairy tale that
nobody stops to think that they might not be the definition of
happiness. Meredith knew that already. We got to the point in the
season when Meredith said, "I can live without you, but I don't

want to," which for any woman is a very powerful statement. It means, "You complement me, but you don't complete me."

Ellen Pompeo All of a sudden, Patrick leaves and it's like, "Oh my God, Meredith's gonna get killed with Alzheimer's." The show couldn't possibly go on without the man!

Shonda Rhimes It was really about allowing her to stand on her own two feet to figure out who she is and to make it more about her career, not who she is going to date. Ellen had strong feelings about that. I do have strong feelings about any one of my female characters basing her existence on whether or not she has a man, and so it's not really about proving whether or not she can exist without a man.

Ellen Pompeo Let's keep it real for a second. This is really difficult for my ego. Because it's like, Annalise Keating carries the show. Olivia Pope carries the show. Why can't I just be the lead of the show? Why can't I be on that [*Grey's Anatomy*] poster by myself?

Pompeo became determined to create a new narrative for ABC's most popular show. She announced on The Ellen De- Generes Show *how "it's amazing how much you get done without a penis" and worked to improve the show's culture behind the scenes. "It became my goal to have an experience there that I could be happy and proud about, because we had so much turmoil for ten years," she told* Variety *in 2019. "My mission became: This can't be fantastic to the public and a disaster behind the scenes. Shonda Rhimes and I decided to rewrite the ending of this story. That's what kept me. Patrick Dempsey left the show in season eleven, and the studio and*

*network believed the show could not go on without the male
lead. So I had a mission to prove that it could."*

Tony Phelan Everybody's entitled to their own opinion.

Jeannine Renshaw I have to say that I actually believe that
one hundred percent, because I was there for the first ten years.
I think that's incredibly insightful. After that ten years, when
she had her epiphany, it became more of a team and she was
the leader, for sure. The captain. When I was there, that was for
sure not happening.

Jenna Bans Sure, it was challenging and certain personalities were more challenging than other ones. But it was nothing
so out of the norm of what I've experienced on other shows. So
for me, I wouldn't have used those words [that it was "a disaster"], but again, everybody has their own experience. Ellen was
in the trenches. I mean, she worked a lot. We would shoot for
nine days, and she probably worked eight of those. She was in a
ton of scenes. I know that they made a lot of changes throughout the years just in terms of directors and different producers
on set, and I know that seemed to make, from what I hear, people happier in the later years.

Norman Leavitt As it became her show, she blossomed. I'm
so proud of her. It got easier for her because she was recognized. She was better at her job.

Jeannine Renshaw Ellen is a strong, powerful woman who
stands up for what she believes and speaks her mind. We had a
lot of arguments on set, but I always felt she had a valid point.
I felt like we could argue as equals. She definitely had her opinions. If there was a line she didn't want to say, she was very

vocal about it. It would sometimes become a public fight where I would say, "Can we talk about this in private?" I've probably had more of my tense arguments with her, but I left respecting her one hundred percent. She would definitely shoot people down if they were complaining and say, "Hey, we're all here together. We're all doing it together." In that way she was a leader. She tried to keep things fair and keep things going. I remember when Ellen's dad had just passed and she was working. I was like, "Why are you even at work?" She was like, "I have to be here." She was such a trooper.

Kate Burton Ellen has been obviously so wonderfully great on this show as an actress. It's been a beautiful experience to watch her gorgeous work. But she's also broken the mold in that not only is she an actress on the show but she's also a businessperson, and it's great. It's great for all actors and actresses making their way and navigating the murk.

*It still took Pompeo a while to get over how fans seemed to value Dempsey more than her. The issue came up in 2015 when Pompeo joined Rhimes, Viola Davis (*How to Get Away with Murder*), and Kerry Washington (*Scandal*) for an* Entertainment Weekly *cover shoot to celebrate Shondaland's success.*

Melissa Maerz (Former *EW* Senior Writer) I interviewed Shonda Rhimes, Ellen Pompeo, Kerry Washington, and Viola Davis for the cover story of *Entertainment Weekly* in September 2015. When I showed up for the interview, the four of them had just done a photo shoot, and the energy in the room was kind of strange. I won't pretend to know what was going on, whether the politics of the photo shoot were complicated by the fact that there were three series leads on the same cover or whether it was just a very long day on set. But before we sat down, Pompeo seemed a bit jittery and anxious. Everyone else seemed pretty calm. Most of the women still had their cover-shoot makeup and hair, which always looks a little over-the-top and costume-y and unreal, especially when you're looking at it behind the scenes. But when Davis walked into the room for the interview, she had taken off her makeup and her cover-shoot dress and she was just wearing a simple robe and a black head wrap. I was immediately drawn to her. That felt like such a sign of strength, to show up for an interview completely stripped of all the usual armor. She might've just been more comfortable that way, but to me, the choice felt intentional. She had just had this incredibly powerful moment on her show, *How to Get Away with Murder,* when her character takes off her makeup and her wig before confronting her husband, and the scene had been her idea. She'd told *Essence* that being fully made-up on the show made her feel like something "not human," and she'd said part of being human, as a Black woman, was taking your hair off at night, and she wanted the world to see that. Having her show up that way for the interview was powerful. It was like, Oh, okay, we're going to talk about TV, but we're also going to have a deeper conversation here.

I knew I wanted to talk to all of them about sexism and racism in Hollywood. It's a huge understatement to say that there weren't many women showrunners or Black showrunners on network TV at that time, much less a Black woman like Rhimes who was running or executive producing three successful shows at the same time, so I wanted to hear about what Rhimes's experience had been like as an outlier in the industry and how she had been viewed and treated by others. My first question for the three actresses was, "What was your first impression of Shonda?" Pompeo was the first to answer, which made sense, since she had known Rhimes the longest. But her response made everyone squirm. She said she got along with Rhimes not only because they were the same age and she trusted Rhimes's vision but also because Rhimes was a Black woman. Pompeo's exact quote was, "I always feel comfortable around Black people." Washington and Davis laughed. It was an eye-roll kind of laugh. But Pompeo doubled down and added, "My husband's Black!"

Looking back, I regret not challenging her. I didn't have a lot of time left in the interview, and I wanted to give the other three women a chance to talk. I asked Washington and Davis if it felt like a different experience for them to work for a Black woman. They both said it was. What followed was a really rich conversation between Davis, Rhimes, and Washington. They talked about internalized misogyny among female TV executives, how colorism is still at work in casting, the idea that Hollywood thinks you have to talk a certain way and come from Detroit or Atlanta in order to qualify as being Black, and you can't, as Davis put it, come from Central Falls, Rhode Island, and listen to John Denver.

The conversation turned to Alessandra Stanley, a TV critic at *The New York Times* who had written a racist review of *How to Get Away with Murder*, in which she said that Davis was not "classically beautiful" and suggested that Rhimes's biography should be called *How to Get Away with Being an Angry Black Woman*. There was a swift backlash against Stanley—rightfully so—and a good conversation about it on Twitter. I asked Rhimes and Davis if they felt anything positive had come out of that backlash. Rhimes was in the middle of answering when Pompeo said, "If any good comes out of ignorance, then I'll take ignorance."

It was a total record-scratch moment. Was she really saying that if any good came out of racism, then racism was okay with her? And why was Pompeo even responding to a question that had nothing to do with her or her show? Everyone was totally silent, and then I heard Davis let out a long, deep sigh. I asked her what she thought of what Pompeo said. "I understand what Ellen is talking about," she said. "But I've been on the other side of ignorance." Pompeo's eyes welled up with tears, and she got up and left the room.

If I had to guess, I'd say that Ellen immediately regretted what she said and didn't want to draw too much attention to herself by crying in front of the others. But it ended up being even more distracting to have her stand up and walk out, diverting attention from Davis, who was in the middle of saying something important. To her credit, Davis calmly continued after Pompeo left. She said, "Colorism and racism in this country are so powerful that the Jim Crow laws are gone, but what's left is a mindset. As an actress, I have been a great victim of that." Responding to Stanley's comment about her not being classically beautiful, she talked about the types of roles she has not been allowed to play as a fifty-year-old dark-skinned woman and how exciting it was to finally get to play a character whose sexuality was central to who she was.

Pompeo soon returned to the room, and everyone was extremely gracious to her when she did. Washington even patted her back and asked if she was all right. But the whole thing was very disruptive. There were four very smart, successful women in the room, talking about racism and sexism in Hollywood and whether it was intentional or not, but Pompeo kept making the interview about her.

Since Pompeo always seemed to suggest she was thisclose to quitting, it always came as a surprise when announcements were made that she'd signed on for more seasons. Even back in 2007, Pompeo was questioning whether the show had the legs to make it to an eighth year on ABC.

Ellen Pompeo I don't know how you come up with original material for that long. To keep the same audience for eight years? I don't know how likely that is. You know, it's human nature of change, evolution. You don't want to wear the same dress every summer. After three or four summers you're like, "Oh, give this dress to Goodwill," or, "Give it to my niece or whatever you want to do." It's just human nature to want change.

But in January 2018, Pompeo signed a new pact that, at more than $570,000 per episode, would make her TV's highest-paid dramatic actress. Pompeo's talent agency convinced her that ABC/Disney could more than afford to give *her a $20 million deal, since* Grey's Anatomy *was a billion-dollar franchise that aired in more than two hundred territories throughout the world.*

Ellen Pompeo Women approached me on the street in tears, crying, and it's really interesting how as women we are really not used to, or accustomed to, being forceful and asking for what we want, or asking for what we deserve, or speaking up, or speaking our mind. It's been a very interesting ride, the whole topic of standing up for yourself and what it takes to get yourself emotionally to the place where you're comfortable doing that. Of course, it was a challenging thing to do right, because I'm in a very specific situation. Like I had said in the past, I had very quantifiable numbers that I could derive my number from. Not everybody has the blessing to be able to do that. You don't know how your work impacts your workplace. It's hard to quantify what you do in your workplace and how does that result in numbers. I'm very fortunate where I actually do get to see how my presence directly impacts the money that the show makes.

Finally, Pompeo learned how to embrace her new role as ABC's most valuable star. She stopped working on Fridays, gained a wicked sense of humor (at one point BuzzFeed wrote a story about the "16 Times Ellen Pompeo Gave Absolutely Zero Fucks on Twitter"), and became an outspoken social advocate—even if it meant criticizing someone on her own network. In 2019, she targeted The Bachelor *creator Mike Fleiss after he dinged Kelly Ripa for ripping his show.*

"Your show does NOT pay @Kelly Ripa salary," she tweeted. "Also, we don't attack successful women on our network and men certainly cannot take credit for their success. Don't get me started on your show cuz I'm a savage." She ended it with #bachelorsoooowhite. She was also unabashed about how difficult it is to age on-screen. "You really see [the difference] because I'm in the same clothes [playing] the same character," she told the Armchair Expert *podcast. "So the way I see myself aging, it's a motherfucker." At the age of fifty, Pompeo became one of the most relatable women on TV.*

Ellen Pompeo I have definitely played this out for everything that I possibly could. I've given it two hundred percent of my energy and my love and my time and my commitment and my dedication. I still am fighting every day for the quality to be good, for the actors to be happy. I still care very much about the show.

There's a story about how Ilee and Vera Rhimes—Shonda's parents—tried to visit the Grey's Anatomy *set once but couldn't get past the guard gate. As legend has it, Mama Rhimes leaned over her husband in the driver's seat and yelled, "Shonda Rhimes came out of my vagina. You let me in this set!" He must have waved them through, since there were never subsequent reports of a missing security guard at Prospect Studios. Shonda Rhimes may have lacked experience when she first launched* Grey's Anatomy, *but no one ever doubted her strength and resolve (qualities, it seems, that ran in the family). From the very beginning, everyone knew they were in the presence of someone special.*

Kate Burton Shonda was a very, very young woman when I first met her. I didn't realize, actually, how young she was.

Eric Buchman If Shonda was stressed out, she did a very good job of hiding it. I was always super impressed by how quickly she grew into the role of not just TV showrunner but an empire runner. Like, she seemed prepared for almost everything. And I've worked on a number of shows with a number of showrunners who have way more experience than her. There was nothing that would have given away the fact that this was her very first TV show. She came from a feature world, so I think that was one of the reasons why people were constantly thinking she might be able to pick this up quickly.

Tony Phelan She had, from the beginning, such a clear idea. And to ABC's credit, they let her keep to her vision. Because anyone else would have said, "If you make that decision for that character, the audience is not going to like that character anymore."

Peter Horton We talked a lot about what makes projects really work in television, which is emotion much more than anything. If you can describe emotion in an intimate, honest way, even if it involves guys on a cop show or people in a hospital, people will respond to it. She and I came to that touchstone. She really knew how to [write] a romance.

Mark Saul She was very focused. She would usually go outside to write and get in her own zone. There was a picnic table at Prospect Studios and she would sit with her headphones on. She would come back with a really neat script or two.

Jenna Bans I can picture her to this day with those Bose headphones that blocked out all noise. She just liked to be outside, and she would sit there with her laptop, writing.

Nicole Rubio You'd see her with her hair parted down the middle, with two Afro puffs, sitting there writing outside the writers' bungalow. You knew not to bother her.

Stephen McPherson I love Shonda because she's a lot like me: no bullshit, straightforward. She would fight me on things that she was passionate about, what she believed in.

Tony Phelan The other joy of *Grey's Anatomy* is that we just love those people and continue to be friends with the cast and crew and everybody. The thing that she should get a lot more credit for is her incredible ability to spot talent and to create this great group of people who can realize her vision.

From the beginning, Rhimes endeared herself to her actresses when it came time to film one of the many sex scenes in Grey's. She left it up to the women to decide how much—or how little—skin they wanted to show on camera. As a mother herself, she also accommodated everyone's desire to start families.

Sarah Drew If I didn't want to be in a bra, like, I would rather be in a lacy tank top, she was like, "Sure, fine, cool, let's do it." Nobody shamed you, nobody made you feel bad about it, nobody tried to pressure you into anything else. We as women were protected and cared for [in] those scenes, but also as mothers because so many of us had babies on that show. We were just really being taken care of in that regard.

Mimi Melgaard There was a lotta babies. Sarah Drew had two. Jessica had three, Caterina had two. And it seems like they're always pregnant during the wedding stuff. When Amelia married Owen, we wanted a dress that was soft but plain. We knew that she had to get wet [from the rain], so we were like, "It has to be something that can get soaking wet but will look decent afterwards." I knew she was pregnant, but she wasn't showing a lot. We shot it at the end of season twelve. We come back after hiatus and she's showing a lot, and they had all these new scenes they wanted to shoot. It was like, "That dress isn't going to fit anymore. She's pregnant!" So we had to get another dress, much bigger, and hide her belly with some dancing. It's the same dress, it's just much bigger. If you really look at [the season thirteen premiere], you can see her body shape is different. There's always those little pregnancy things you're hiding. Jessica had lots of them. She was a pro at carrying a purse or an X-ray. She also put her hands in her lab coat pockets and stuck her hands out so it made a little partition on the sides. You couldn't see her belly.

Long before the push for more diversity became a priority in Hollywood, Rhimes pioneered what was once called "color-blind casting"—even though it sometimes irked her when too much attention was paid to how she routinely cast persons of color in major roles. In 2014, Rhimes admitted that she and Beers "were disappointed" when the Directors Guild of America presented her with a Diversity Award. "While I'm still really and truly profoundly honored to receive this award . . . we're a little pissed off because there still needs to be an award," she said at the DGA ceremony.

*"Like, there's such a lack of people hiring women and mi-
norities that when someone does on a regular basis, they are
given an award."*

Shonda Rhimes I'm a Black woman casting my own show.
I wanted their world to look like the world that I live in. I don't
think about it in those terms [diversity], and I militantly think
I don't have to.

Isaiah Washington We [tried] to give our characters levels
and not just be the taboo people of color screwing.

*Rhimes also looked for opportunities to tell inclusive stories,
starting with how Meredith's mom suffered from Alzheimer's
disease. It was an unprecedented plot point for a broadcast
network show.*

Kate Burton Anybody who had Alzheimer's in their family
was like, "Oh my God, oh my God, thank you for telling the
story." That scene [in the pilot, when viewers first learn about
Ellis's condition] became one of the indelible scenes. I've been
to a few Alzheimer's benefits. They often show that scene because it was the first time that a character with Alzheimer's was
portrayed on network television.

*Rhimes had something big in store for Dr. April Kepner, even
though it didn't happen until season eight.*

Sarah Drew I remember Tony Phelan told me, "Oh, yeah,
we're going to make April a Christian. She's going to be a very

faithful Christian character and it's going to come out after you sleep with Jackson." I was surprised by the whole thing. I had no idea. But I'm a Christian myself and I grew up in the Christian Church and my dad's a pastor. I was excited to represent the community that I grew up in. Shonda told me right off the bat that she wanted to tell a really authentic story about a Christian, so if I had any thoughts or ideas or if something doesn't feel right, let her know. That was a really cool opportunity for me to participate in the shaping of my character's faith journey.

In 2017, Rhimes cast Sophia Ali as the show's first hijabi surgeon.

Sophia Ali A lot of organizations reached out to me, and it was a very positive response. Everyone was like, "This is so accurate. This is so cool that the hijab is being depicted this way," because in that culture it is very much an accessory. Obviously there are levels of faith, just like with Christianity. A lot of women use it as a form of keeping their anonymity, especially if someone's a doctor. People are very fixated on looks in reality. Everyone's just very superficial. Even for Dahlia, she probably would've had a lot of struggles with her looks as a doctor and people not thinking she could be good because she is good-looking. The hijab adds this veil of secretness. It just hides you a little bit more.

A year later, Alex Landi joined as the show's first gay and Asian male surgeon.

Krista Vernoff I looked at a dozen tapes and [Alex] was the only one where I said, "I need to work with him. I want to meet him because this story line is going to be a big deal." He flew in from New York, and in the casting room I said, "So how long are you in town?" And he said, "I only bought a one-way ticket." And I was like, That's my guy. Just the confidence, it was just great.

Alex Landi (Dr. Nico Kim) Obviously me being half Korean, the Korean and Asian community has been very excited to see the first male Asian surgeon. Sandra Oh was the last surgeon of Asian descent, and I feel truly blessed to take that on.

> *Though she was an instinctive storyteller, Rhimes was a constant work in progress when it came to managing her ever-growing production company. She explained in* Year of Yes *that she learned to lay strict boundaries, like ending all emails with a stern "Please note: I will not engage in work emails after 7 p.m. or on weekends. IF I AM YOUR BOSS, MAY I SUGGEST: PUT DOWN YOUR PHONE." She also was very blunt with her writers and producers.*

Jeannine Renshaw When she doesn't like something of yours, you could just wither. That was the thing about being on the *Grey's* staff. I think that's what made you survive. If you could survive that withering feeling that you experienced with her . . .

Mark Tinker I can remember on the first episode I did, being in the editing room and we were talking about a scene. I outlined the idea I had for the scene and I could see her eyes kind of glazing over. I looked at her and I said, "You're not gonna do any of that, are you?" She said, "No." I said, "Okay. That's fine, no problem." She knew what she was doing, she knew what she wanted. She was very clear about it.

Jeannine Renshaw I remember that first pitch to Shonda. I'd never pitched to Shonda before. I'm standing up, I've got all my story lines on this huge board. I was building to the moment where Scott asked Teddy to marry him. He gets down on his knees, pulls out a ring, and asks her to marry him. Everyone in the room loved that pitch. I remember she looks at me after I was done and goes, "I'm throwing up in my mouth." I remember my feeling of, *I could either die right now or go run and hide in a corner. What are my options here?* Instead, I was like, "Wait a second. No, I'll tell you why it's so great. It's so great because all the stuff that's been happening with Teddy and Scott, we know he's dying." I re-pitch it and she goes, "Ugh, now my eyeballs are bleeding." Thank God I didn't run away. I was like, *Okay, she hates my guts, but I'm just gonna keep going.* In retrospect, it was just not the time for him to ask her to marry him. It hadn't been earned, and in *Grey's* I really learned everything has to be earned.

Mark Wilding She was very direct. If something bored her, she'd ask, "Why are you trying to ruin my show?" You have to have a thick skin. You have to think, What's behind the comment? Is she right or wrong? Let's try to make it better. You cannot take those things to heart, because if you do, you'd curl up in a ball and not come out for ten years.

Jeannine Renshaw She'll even write in one of my scripts that "the lambs are screaming, make it stop." I don't even know what that means, but I know it's not good.

Mark Wilding That was one of her favorites, yeah. She would write on scripts, "This makes my eyes bleed," or she would write, "I hear the lambs screaming."

Harry Werksman Shonda really knew what she wanted. Every script passed through her computer at some point for a final pass. Something that you wrote that you loved wouldn't survive, but you'd be like, "Okay, well, I understand that." But she never took credit away from anyone, no matter how much of a polish she did on a script.

Jeannine Renshaw She'll also write me a note after reading that same script and say, "I love this so much I want to marry it." She's an open raw nerve. She's very genuine, very authentic, and you always know what she's thinking.

Maybe not always. *Over the course of my twenty years at* Entertainment Weekly, *I have interviewed Rhimes several times about* Grey's Anatomy—*but only one encounter stands out, and it had nothing to do with MerDer or the latest actor to join the show. It was in 2015, when EW threw a party for Rhimes and the rest of ABC's TGIT [Thank God It's Thursday] lineup at Gracias Madre restaurant in West Hollywood, California. Rhimes had published her memoir,* Year of Yes, *and she also just went through a personal transformation that included losing a significant amount of weight. She looked terrific, and I was eager to tell her. As soon as she and her small posse found a seat on the patio, I made a beeline for her and paid her the compliment. She responded by staring at me in complete silence. I felt like I had made a huge mistake, so I mumbled something about having*

a good time and skulked away. I already knew Rhimes was a
tough nut to crack; interviewing her was always a challenge
because she was shy and didn't like giving things away about
her show. And unlike some showrunners in town, Rhimes
never seemed too interested in cultivating relationships with
the press—at least not with me. She was both awe-inspiring
and more than a little intimidating.

Jeannine Renshaw I've got to say that I'm sure that as far as
she's concerned, it didn't even register. I doubt it was a big deal
for her. She's strong.

Jennifer Armstrong I feel like Shonda was pretty measured
during the time I was talking to her, too. Like, she was nice and
funny and smart, but it was similar to Ellen in that I think they
all understand what was happening and it was huge. Then it
becomes, "Let's not fuck this up by saying something wrong to
a reporter."

Shonda Rhimes My first season of *Grey's*, I didn't believe
that anybody could fire me, so I behaved like somebody who
couldn't be fired. I was fortunate because I was raised by parents who didn't allow the idea that somebody was going to
make me feel like I wasn't able to do something.

No chance of that. By 2017, Rhimes had five shows either
on ABC or in the works: Grey's Anatomy, Scandal, How
to Get Away with Murder, For the People, *and* Station
19. *She was to ABC what Dick Wolf was to NBC; her shows*
had reportedly generated more than $2 billion in revenue
from advertising, rerun sales, and international licensing.

That's why Rhimes became the first female showrunner ever to grace the cover of Entertainment Weekly.

Henry Goldblatt She's as big of a star as the three women who led her giant TGIT shows. She had this amazing brand. She's one of the first Black showrunners to begin with, not to mention the first Black showrunner to have three hit shows on one network.

Former High-Level Disney Source Shonda was the biggest office at ABC Studios and the ABC television network. People treated her as such. That doesn't mean she got everything she wanted. She was treated with incredible deference and respect, which is what she deserved.

So it was particularly shocking when Netflix announced it had lured Rhimes away from ABC for a multiyear deal worth almost $150 million, not including incentives that could make her even wealthier. ABC, by contrast, was paying Rhimes around $10 million annually—with time still left on her deal. The network/studio released Rhimes early so that she, Beers, and her roughly thirty employees could move to the streamer.

Former High-Level Disney Source It was sort of assumed that if we could make the right deal, she wanted to stay. We were negotiating a deal for her to stay. It was right at the beginning of when Netflix was starting to make those big deals, but it hadn't tipped yet in the sense that everybody was leaving network television.

But a decision was made at the corporate level to cut back
on the offer, given Shondaland's recent failures with The
Catch *(a sexy caper with Mireille Enos and Peter Krause)*
and Still Star-Crossed *(a* Romeo and Juliet *sequel). There*
were also the sobering economic realities facing broadcast TV
and whether any show creator, Rhimes included, would ever
be able to match the success of Grey's Anatomy.

Executive Familiar with the ABC Negotiation In that moment in time, it didn't make sense to put that big of a percentage
of the overall development budget in the hands of one person.
None of this takes away from her success. She's phenomenal.

Former ABC Insider She did a lot of shows for us that
didn't work, which people don't really write about.

Stephen McPherson I don't know why anyone would stay
at a network in today's world. That is not a knock on anyone,
just the reality. I can't think of a reason she would stay.

Shonda Rhimes Shondaland's move to Netflix is the result
of a shared plan [Netflix chief content officer] Ted Sarandos
and I built based on my vision for myself as a storyteller and
for the evolution of my company. Ted provides a clear, fearless
space for creators at Netflix. He understood what I was looking for . . . the opportunity to build a vibrant new storytelling
home for writers with unique creative freedom and instantaneous global reach provided by Netflix's singular sense of in-
novation. The future of Shondaland has limitless possibilities.

Channing Dungey (Former ABC Entertainment Group
President) Over time, there have been people saying, "How are
they going to survive without Aaron Spelling?" "How are they

going to survive without Steven Bochco?" "How are they going to survive without J. J. Abrams?" Now they're saying, "How are they going to survive without Shonda Rhimes?" The great thing is, there's always new talent that emerges. This is going to give them an opportunity to step into the spotlight.

Dungey never got the chance to meet that new talent for ABC; she was removed from her post as entertainment president in November 2018 and replaced by Karey Burke. (She briefly reunited with Rhimes a month later as the vice president of original content at Netflix before leaving to take over as chairman of Warner Bros. Television Group in early 2021.) In the meantime, ABC learned to rely less and less on Shondaland programs: Scandal *wrapped its seven-season run in 2018 with an average of 7.4 million viewers, while the six-year-old* How to Get Away with Murder *said goodbye the following year with 4.2 million.* For the People, *Rhimes's legal drama, never made it to a third season, since it barely cracked 3 million viewers in its second year. As for Netflix, it waited three years before getting its first series from Shondaland.* Bridgerton, *an adaptation of the romance novels set in Regency England by Julia Quinn, debuted at the end of 2020. While promoting her new Netflix show in October of that year, Rhimes got one last dig in about her former Disney bosses during an interview with* The Hollywood Reporter. *She said the final straw to her leaving was when a high-level executive quipped, "Don't you have enough?" when she asked for an extra all-inclusive pass to Disneyland so her sister could attend the amusement park*

with her nanny and kids. "I felt like I was dying," she told
THR. "Like I'd been pushing the same ball up the same hill
in the exact same way for a really long time."

Executive Familiar with the ABC Negotiation I think history has shown it was the right decision [to let Rhimes go]. It freed up development moneys for new voices. It freed up development moneys for alternative types of programming. That in hindsight was a good move, because those are the kinds of programs that are performing well on broadcast. In the last three years, since she's been gone, name me one broadcast network drama that is culturally relevant. [I can! *This Is Us* on NBC. But I'll let the suit make his point.] You can name *The Masked Singer*, you can name a bunch of nonscripted stuff. But dramas on broadcast networks have become an endangered species.

To say Rhimes had the last laugh would be an understatement:
Bridgerton went on to become Netflix's biggest series ever,
watched by a record eighty-two million households around the
world in the first month of its release.

CHAPTER 14

"Everybody Wants Their Place in History," Or, Deciding When to Hang up the Scrubs

At the time this book went to press, *Grey's Anatomy* was film-ing a record-breaking seventeenth season on ABC—in the middle of a global pandemic, no less—and Ellen Pompeo's contract was set to expire in June 2021. If her October 2020 comments to *Variety* were any indication, that should have been her last month on the job. "The truth is, this year could be it," she said. "I don't take this decision lightly. We employ a lot of people, and we have a huge platform. And I'm very grateful for it."

Contingencies were made for a possible Pompeo-free fu-ture: fan favorites Kevin McKidd (Dr. Owen Hunt), Camilla Luddington (Dr. Jo Wilson), and Kim Raver (Dr. Teddy Altman) signed new pacts during the summer of 2020 that would keep them on the show through a potential season eighteen, at least, or for a possible spinoff. But ABC would first have to decide whether it wanted to stick with a series that had lost its title character. As of June 2020, then ABC Entertainment Group president Karey Burke was certainly sounding hopeful: she told *Deadline* that "we'd like it to be part of our schedule for as long as they are interested in making more episodes." But that's an obvious reaction, since broadcast networks never want to cancel popular shows—even if they average only 9.4 million viewers (which was the average audience size for *Grey's* during the 2019–2020 season). CBS, for example, would have loved more seasons of *The Big Bang Theory*—but Jim Parsons put the kibosh on that. As I reported exclusively for *EW* in August 2018, Parsons didn't want to make a thirteenth season of TV's most-watched comedy, and creator Chuck Lorre couldn't imagine a show without him. So *TBBT* ended in 2019, after twelve years.

The expiration date of *Grey's Anatomy* has been a source of speculation for years—both on and off the set. Even showrunner Krista Vernoff told *Variety* in October 2020 that "we've blown past so many potential endings to *Grey's Anatomy* that I always assume it can go on forever." But some actors started behaving years earlier as though the job had become the equivalent of simply punching a clock.

Tom Burman I'll never forget what I heard on the pilot. I don't remember whom this actress was talking to, but she was saying, "I just feel so blessed that I finally have this series, and this is going to be so wonderful." Then, cut to years later, and

I hear her telling the makeup artist, "You know, they want me to come in on Saturday for a lousy $128,000. I told them to go to hell. I'm not gonna come in Saturday." And I'm thinking, Really? You're telling this makeup artist, who at that time was probably making, I don't know, $35 an hour, you're not gonna come in on Saturday for $128,000? That kind of became the attitude. I mean, I loved those guys. But some of them started to buy in to their own importance.

Jeff Melman At first, the actors were very easy to work with, and they were very trusting. Then I remember in a later episode when I went into the first assistant director's office and she was writing notes on a legal pad and looking at her computer schedule. She was looking up and down and writing and checking. I asked, "What is that list on your legal pad?" She said, "Well, these are the days that the actors can't be here." So at that point they were deciding what days they wanted to work and what days they didn't. I wasn't a fan of that.

Stacy McKee It's so funny, because I feel like for years, almost every year, we were like, "Oh, this is probably the last season." Nope, it's not. It just keeps going. It's crazy.

Sarah Drew I didn't ever think, Oh, the show won't go on, or anything like that, because it's such an ensemble show. So many characters have left and died, but it's still going on.

Matt Mania I am [surprised it is still on]. It's one of those things where, if people hear I worked on *Grey's Anatomy*, they'll ask, "Is that show still on?" or say, "Yeah, my girlfriend watches that show." Those are the two answers you get.

Stephen McPherson It's just surprising, given normal

television cycles. It's just a long time to keep things going. But it seems like they've done a good job of it. I think it's great that Shonda has been able to preserve that show.

Rhimes has her newest employer to thank for that. In 2010, Netflix acquired prior seasons of Grey's Anatomy, which not only boosted the subscriber base for the streaming service but brought a whole new generation of viewers to the ABC show.

Patrick Dempsey Multiple generations have discovered Derek through Netflix. They are passionate around the world. I get to travel around the world to race, and people know who Shepherd is. It's humbling.

Nicole Rubio The show has been on so many years that the audience recycles itself. I don't know when it's going to end. I think I read somewhere where Shonda said, "If Ellen doesn't want to do it anymore, then we'll stop." The masses love Meredith Grey. I bet you some of them feel like, "If Meredith goes, then I'm done."

Peter Horton It's one of my favorite stories: I have two daughters, who are now twenty and seventeen, who grew up on the set of *Grey's*. They'd come down and visit me when they were little kids, but I couldn't get them to watch it. Then it got discovered on Netflix, so all their friends started discovering. We got lucky. *Grey's* started to get to its expiration date right when Netflix revived it.

It's been some time since Rhimes focused on Grey's Anatomy. At the start of season fourteen, she passed the show-runner duties to Vernoff, who together with Debbie Allen has worked hard to change the culture on the set. "Nobody should be working sixteen hours a day, ten months a year, nobody," Pompeo told Variety in October 2020. "And it's just causing people to be exhausted, pissed, sad, depressed. It's a really, really unhealthy model. And I hope post-COVID-19 nobody ever goes back to twenty-four or twenty-two episodes a season. It's why people get sick. It's why people have break-downs. It's why actors fight! You want to get rid of a lot of bad behavior? Let people go home and sleep."

Shonda Rhimes I was doing the day-to-day for almost thir-teen seasons, so there was a level of exhaustion like, "This has been a marathon." It was surprisingly hard at the beginning. I thought I would feel a little relieved to have a break, but in the be-ginning it was really hard. But then it felt really good, because the show was really good. I think it would have been difficult if I had pulled back and then I didn't like what was coming out. Krista was there for the first seven seasons, so it's been a real experience for me to actually go, as they say, "send a kid off to college." I don't think that I could be a person who sat and just signed off on every script, because if I allow myself to have input, then I'm going to have notes, and if I have notes, then everybody has to take my notes. Krista is the only person that I've ever known who has my sensibility and understands the voice of what I've always been say-ing about the show. It's been really exciting to let her run with it.

Tony Phelan The actors need one person they can go to, talk about their character, talk about the script, to know they have a willing ear in somebody who can communicate to the writers' room their concerns and their excitement or their questions or whatever. You want somebody who can effortlessly move between those two worlds. Debbie Allen has that job now. I think the success of any show is based on having that line of communication really work.

> *But Rhimes and Pompeo will definitely have a say in when and how the show will end. There had been talk at one point that Alex Karev would play a big role in the show's goodbye; that obviously had to change after Justin Chambers left the show. But Rhimes and Vernoff certainly love a good comeback: besides Dempsey's much-heralded return in season seventeen, Knight came back as George while Drew, as April, swooped in to see Jackson. With so many heart-stopping reunions, how could we not assume season seventeen was going to be the last for* Grey's Anatomy? *Or maybe she dies from COVID-19 and reunites with Derek on the beach.*

Krista Vernoff I will say that we have been building this [seventeenth] season from the beginning as if it's the last season. The reason why you're like, "Oh my gosh" every episode is because we approached it with a certain reverence of "Okay, if this is the last season and we're doing COVID, what are we doing?"

Shonda Rhimes I have written the end of the show at least six times. But we just don't end. Every time I thought, This is how the show should end, we've gone past those moments, so I've stopped trying. I'm incredibly proud of the show and I still, every day, pinch myself that we even got on the air and that people watch and care about it as much as they do. I think everything about that show has been a miracle to me.

Entertainment Weekly Sources

"Dr. Oh," by Jennifer Armstrong, April 1, 2005

"Amazing *Grey's*," June 24/July 1, 2005

"Anatomy of a Shakeup," by Lynette Rice, March 30, 2018

"Playing Doctors," by Nicholas Fonseca, September 23, 2005

"*Grey's Anatomy*," fall preview story, by Jennifer Armstrong, September 8, 2006

"5 Things You Should Know About Sara Ramirez," by Vanessa Juarez, November 10, 2006

"The Cast of *Grey's Anatomy*," Entertainers of the Year, by Jennifer Armstrong, December 29, 2006

"ABC's Rx for Success," by Lynette Rice, March 9, 2007

"Baby, It's You," by Karen Valby, June 8, 2007

"Washington Speaks Out," by Paul Katz, June 22, 2007

"*Private Practice* Starring Kate Walsh," by Lynette Rice, September 14, 2007

"*Grey's Anatomy* Fall TV Preview," by Lynette Rice, September 14, 2007

"Pick Me Choose Me Love Me," by Lynette Rice, May 9, 2008

"Heigl Kicks Wienie," by Mark Harris, July 25, 2008

"Fall TV Preview," by Lynette Rice, September 12, 2008

"The Ausiello Files," by Michael Ausiello, November 14, 2008

"The Doctor Is Out," by Michael Ausiello, July 31, 2009

"Katherine Heigl: The Goodbye Girl," by Michael Ausiello, April 2, 2010

"How *Grey's* Got Its Groove Back," by Jennifer Armstrong, April 1, 2011

"Jeffrey Dean Morgan," by Lynette Rice, April 6, 2012

"Farewell, Mark Sloan," by Shonda Rhimes, October 12/19, 2012

"*Private Practice*'s Kate Walsh," by Lynette Rice, January 25, 2013

"Graceful Exit Sandra Oh," by Sandra Gonzalez, May 9, 2014

"Inside Burke's Return," by Sandra Gonzalez, May 1, 2014

"Farewell, Cristina," by Sandra Gonzalez, December 1, 2014

"The Doctor Is . . . Out," by Lynette Rice, May 1, 2015

"The Anatomy of How to Get Away with Scandalously Good TV," by Melissa Maerz, September 11, 2015

"Sara Ramirez Exits After 10 Years as Callie Torres," by Natalie Abrams, May 23, 2016

"Shonda Rhimes Addresses Sara Ramirez' Exit," by Joey Nolfi, May 23, 2016

"Shonda Rhimes Jumps ABC Ship to Netflix," by Natalie Abrams, August 14, 2017

"*Grey's Anatomy* Goes Three Rounds at *EW* Popfest," hosted by Henry Goldblatt, October 30, 2016

"*Grey's Anatomy:* The Body Bomb," by Lynette Rice, April 7/14, 2017

"Jerrika Hinton Leaves Shondaland," by Natalie Abrams, May 18, 2017

"The Real Stories Behind the Craziest (and Grossest) Medical Cases," by Ruth Kinane, September 25, 2018

"Doctors Without Borders," by Lynette Rice, September 28, 2018

"*Grey's* Producers Break Down THAT Emotional Scene," by Lynette Rice, March 28, 2019

"From *School Ties* to *NCIS: LA:* The Roles of Chris O'Donnell," by Lynette Rice, November 8, 2020

"From *Grey's Anatomy* to *Virgin River:* The Roles of Martin Henderson," by Lynette Rice, November 27, 2020

"Giacomo Gianniotti on his Devastating *Grey's Anatomy* departure," by Ruth Kinane, March 12, 2021

"*Grey's Anatomy* Boss Talks Writing Season 17 'As If It's the Last Season,'" by Samantha Highfill, March 17, 2021

Acknowledgments

Full disclosure: I still get weepy when I rewatch the death of Derek Shepherd. But that's not why I wrote this book. For years, we have done oral histories at *Entertainment Weekly* because it's a fun and breezy way to tell a more complete story about a TV show. So when former editor turned agent Jon Michael Darga emailed me in the spring of 2019 about assembling a *Grey's Anatomy* oral history, I first said, "Seriously?!" (natch) before adding, "You bet!"

Fortunately, then–*Entertainment Weekly* editor in chief Henry Goldblatt was a big fan of the series, so he gave me the green light to pursue the book. Even after he left the magazine, he remained a big champion of the project and was generous with help and suggestions for interviews. Of all the editors I've had in my thirty-year career as a print journalist, he will always be my favorite.

Lucky for me, my former *EW* colleague James Hibberd had sold an oral history of *Game of Thrones* right around the same time I did, so we had each other to lean on when the going got tough. I'm so thankful he was just a Slack message away. And when we weren't crying to each other, we ran to *EW* legend Kristen Baldwin to call us off the ledge. Thank you for being there, Kristen, and always remember that *toilet paper is a luxury, MACGRUBER*.

Speaking of some of the best journalists around, thank you to Michael Ausiello, Jennifer Armstrong, Melissa Maerz, Nicholas Fonseca, Richard Maltz, Lesley Goldberg, and Kristin Dos Santos for sharing their unique experiences on the *Grey's* beat. Didn't we have a ball?

Help with photos came courtesy of the great Michele Romero, another charter member of *EW*'s Hall of Fame. Special thanks to Meredith Corporation's Rachel Podmajersky for helping me obtain the old *EW* covers.

Blessings to all those publicists and managers who made it possible to report this book during the pandemic, especially Matthew Mitchell, Lisa Stein, Beth McClinton, Melissa Kates, April Mills, Myrna Jacoby, Loch Powell, Greg McKay, Hannah Parker, Chelsea Hayes, Jenny Wilson, Lori Jonas, Craig Bankey, Marnie Sparer, Micaela Cohen, Mia Hansen, Lauri Hogan, Tommy Lombardi, Heather Griffith, Natalie Thomas, Nancy Seltzer, Paul Hewitt, Clay Schiebel, Kama Nist, Todd Justice, Patrick Confrey, Sarah Kenney, and Todd Eisner.

I'm not much of a music person—I listen to Audible when I'm in the car—but I was so thrilled when Gary Lightbody of Snow Patrol, Isaac Slade and Joe King of the Fray, and Ingrid Michaelson agreed to talk to me. Those are my favorite chapters from the book. Shonda Rhimes, don't forget to invite these very special people to the *Grey's Anatomy* wrap party.

To my poor husband, Mike, who learned to live with a perpetually stressed-out and terribly moody wife. I owe you a year's supply (okay, maybe five) of Gainey Chardonnay.

Thanks to Mom and Dad for bingeing *Grey's Anatomy* on Netflix while I finished the book. Your love doesn't get any more unconditional than that. To my sister Lynae, a Denny girl if there ever was one. Your support made all the difference in the world.

To Kat and Louie, the most important chapter of my life.

And to my agent and partner in crime, Jon: I couldn't have done it without you. In sentimental moments like this, I prefer to rely on the profound words of Dr. Cristina Yang that were first uttered to Dr. Meredith Grey in Joe's Bar, circa season two: You're my person (in publishing).

Last, I'm so grateful for all the writers, actors, former crew members, and executives who agreed to participate in this book. Everyone spoke with such passion and enthusiasm about the show—even though, at times, it felt as though several of them were holding something back. "It's the story of one of the greatest successes in television history, and the rise of an amazing creator, actors, all that stuff," one person told me. "But to me, the real story is never going to be fully told, because people won't talk—at least on the record, like me."

Index

Names of actors and real people are **boldfaced**.
Names of characters are in lightface.